Ce

Calling

Your Celestial Calling

You Came Here for More Than a Schedule

AYLA REN

RUPA

The views and opinions expressed in this book are the author's own and the facts are as reported by her which have been verified to the extent possible, and the publishers are not in any way liable for the same.

ISBN: 978-93-7003-444-0

First impression 2025

10 9 8 7 6 5 4 3 2 1

FSC www.fsc.org
MIX
Paper | Supporting responsible forestry
FSC® C010615

This book is produced from independently certified FSC® paper to ensure responsible forest management.

Part 3
Stillness, Soul Space
The Deep Ocean of Your Mind

CONTENTS

The meaning of life is to find your gift. The purpose of life is to give it away.”.

—Pablo Picasso

1

THE NOISE YOU MISTOOK FOR PURPOSE

Once you make a decision,
the universe conspires to make it happen.

—Ralph Waldo Emerson

It's 7:00 AM and your alarm rings. Almost instantly, your mind starts running through the ***to-do list*** *for the day. Emails to send, meetings to attend, errands to run—the hustle begins before you've even fully opened your eyes. You rush through your morning routine, maybe gulping down coffee while scrolling through notifications. By midday, you're juggling tasks, replying "Busy, can't talk now" to friends, feeling a strange mix of* ***stress and accomplishment****. Late in the evening, you collapse into bed, exhausted. You've* *been* ***busy*** *since dawn, yet there's a quiet nagging in your heart: Why do I feel so empty?*

Why Being Busy Isn't the Same as Being Aligned

We live in a world that treats *"busy" as a badge of honour*. Ask someone how they are, and you'll often hear, "Good—just so busy." Society has long glorified busyness as something to be proud of. Being busy makes us feel *needed* and *important*, as if a packed schedule alone gives our life meaning. We mistakenly equate activity with purpose, believing that if our calendar isn't full, we're somehow falling behind. But let me ask you this, as one article did pointedly: Is being "busy" really something to take pride in? Does a *hectic schedule* truly equal a meaningful life? Deep down, you probably suspect the answer: No. Being busy is not the same as being fulfiled or aligned with your true purpose.

Alignment is different from mere activity. Alignment is *intentional*. It means your actions stem from your core values and authentic desires, not just from obligations or fear of missing out. When you're aligned, you're doing the things that actually matter to you, that light you up inside, even if your to-do list is shorter. When you're just busy, you might be doing a lot, but none of it nourishes your soul. It's the difference between noise and music—one is a chaotic clamour, the other is a harmonious melody. Many of us have been listening to the noise and mistaking it for music, mistaking all that motion for meaning. Our days are loud with *notifications, tasks, and distractions*, but our inner voice—the one that whispers what truly matters—gets drowned out in the din. *Peace didn't leave us; it was drowned in the noise we mistook for purpose.*

Busy vs. Aligned: What's the Difference?

Let's unpack this by comparing **busy** versus **aligned** in everyday life. Consider these contrasts between a life of *busyness* and a life of *purposeful alignment*:

- Being Busy is about quantity: checking off as many tasks as possible, saying yes to everything, staying in constant motion. Being Aligned is about quality: doing the *right* tasks that resonate with you, even if that means doing less.
- Busy feels like a chase—you're always racing the clock, feeling there's never enough time. Aligned feels like a flow—time tends to *melt away* when you're engaged in meaningful work or moments; you're often surprised at how immersed you became.
- Busy is draining. After a day of busywork, you feel exhausted and perhaps anxious, wondering if you did enough. Aligned is energizing. When

your day includes activities that align with your heart (like a creative project, helping someone, or simply taking a mindful walk), you end the day feeling nourished, even if physically tired.

- Busy is driven by "shoulds" and external expectations. You take on projects because you feel you should—to impress others, to not let someone down, or just out of habit. Aligned is guided by desires and values—you do things because they genuinely matter to you or bring you joy, even if they don't make sense to others.
- Busy wears stress as a status symbol. It says, "Look how *needed* I am!" Aligned embraces peace as a way of being. It says, "I know what's important to me, and I make space for it," without needing to prove anything.

Take a moment to reflect on those comparisons. Does anything ring true for you? Maybe you recognise times in your life when you were just going through the motions, doing *too much*, and yet feeling as if nothing you did truly mattered. Perhaps you've had days where you were hyper-productive on paper, yet at night you felt strangely unfulfiled. That is the telltale sign that you've been caught in **busy-ness** rather than purpose. As one writer noted from personal experience, "*I used to think a packed schedule meant I was significant, until I realised that busyness doesn't equal fulfilment. I* *was chasing the feeling of importance...to prove I was significant.*". In other words, we often use busyness to feed the **ego's need for validation**—to feel important or worthy—but it rarely satisfies for long. It's like eating candy when you're starving; it gives a quick rush but no lasting nourishment.

The Glorification of Busy: How did we get here? Part of it is cultural. From school onward, we're taught to measure our worth by **productivity** and achievements. There's pressure to always be **doing**—get the good grades, the promotions, the accolades. *Free time* can almost induce guilt, as if relaxing means you're lazy or falling behind. We scroll through social media and see everyone else's highlight reels of constant activity—new projects, events, hustle—and feel we have to keep up. Being "busy" starts to feel like the only acceptable state. We subconsciously think, if I'm busy, I'm useful, I'm pulling my weight, I matter.

But here's a gentle wake-up call: **Being busy is not the same as being *important*.** Anyone can fill their day with **activities**, but not all activity is *meaningful*. As an article in *Caring Magazine* put it, being busy just means you've chosen to fill your schedule with commitments—it doesn't automatically grant importance or value to your life. In fact, *anyone* can be busy; all it takes is saying "yes" to a lot of things. But *purposeful alignment*? That's something different. That requires discernment—

sometimes saying "no" to the noise so you can say "yes" to what truly matters.

Consider this: If a stranger looked at your calendar or a log of how you spent your time this week, what would they guess is most important to you? Would your schedule clearly show your **priorities** and passions, or just how busy you are? If your days are filled edge-to-edge with obligations that don't reflect your core values, it might be time to **reconfigure your schedule**. At the end of the day, if your life isn't filled with the things that align with what you truly want and value, you deserve to ask: *What am I busy for?* Life is too precious to spend it on autopilot, checking off tasks that don't lead to growth or joy.

2

THE HIGH COST OF CONSTANT DOING

Don't ask what the world needs. Ask what makes you come alive, and go do it.

—Howard Thurman

When you stay busy just for the sake of being busy, you pay a price. Constant busyness can numb you to your own ***intuition and feelings****. It's as if all that noise and rush creates a static that makes it impossible to tune into the subtle inner whispers guiding you. Have you ever noticed that your best ideas or genuine feelings often surface in moments of quiet—like when you're taking a shower, driving alone without the radio, or enjoying a peaceful moment of coffee? There's a reason for that.* ***Clarity speaks***

in the silence. *When we're constantly occupied, we have no space to hear our inner guidance or notice the gentle nudges life is giving us toward our true path.*

Busy-ness can also become a form of **escape**. This might be hard to admit, but many of us stay busy to avoid facing something. We fear what we might discover in the quiet—maybe feelings of dissatisfaction with our job or relationship, or an inkling that the life we built isn't quite the one we deeply desire. So we keep running on the treadmill of tasks, because if we slow down, even for a moment, those truths might catch up to us. It's like filling every silence in a conversation so you don't have to address the awkward question hanging in the air. In life, the awkward question we avoid might be: *Am I truly happy?* or *What do I really want?* Busy noise drowns out these questions, but they *never* stop quietly knocking.

Physically, the toll of never-ending activity is **burnout**, stress, and fatigue. Emotionally, the toll is feeling *disconnected* from your own life. You might be doing a lot *for* your life, but not really *living* it. Picture a hamster on a wheel—running faster and faster, but not actually *going* anywhere new. Now picture a traveller on a path, sometimes walking, sometimes pausing to rest or look at the map, adjusting course intentionally, and eventually reaching a beautiful destination. In which scenario do you recognise yourself? The hamster or the mindful traveller? If you resonated more with the hamster wheel, don't judge yourself—many of us start there. The key is recognising it so you can step off that wheel and choose a more aligned path.

Redefining Purpose (It's Not a To-Do List)

One of the biggest shifts we can make is **redefining what "purpose" means to us**. Purpose is not just *being productive*. In fact, as a recent Psychology Today article noted, purpose is almost the **opposite** of the modern notion of productivity. Productivity is all about *outcomes*—the product, the result, the checkmarks on a list. Purpose, on the other hand, thrives in the *process*. It's not just about what you do, but *how* you do it and *why* you do it. True purpose is found in doing things that light you up, that feel meaningful in and of themselves, not because they earn you a reward or approval.

Think about someone who loves gardening. A productivity mindset might focus on how many vegetables they harvest (the outcome). A purpose mindset finds joy in the act of gardening itself—feeling the sun, tending to the plants, connecting with nature—regardless of how big the harvest is. In your life, what are the activities that you do simply for the *love of it*? The things where you care about the experience more than any badge or gold star at the end? Those are clues to your purpose. It could be moments of **creative flow**, time spent helping others, learning something new, or nurturing relationships.

On the contrary, when we chase big external goals because we think *achieving* them will finally make us feel worthy or happy, we often end up on a hamster wheel of **endless striving**. You hit one milestone, celebrate for a day, and then ask "What's next?" and push the bar higher. The gratification is fleeting, and you're off chasing the next achievement. It's an unfulfiling cycle because it's never truly *enough*. Purpose isn't a finish line in the distance; it's the path you walk every day. If you're only focused on the finish lines, you miss the whole journey *and* the sense of meaning that could be felt along the way.

So ask yourself: *What if I approached my life as a journey to be savoured, rather than a project to be completed?* Shifting this perspective is at the heart of living in alignment. It's realizing that the **means** (how you live each day) are more important than the ends. Ironically, when you do this, the ends take care of themselves—you tend to create a life that *feels* successful on the inside, not just looks successful on the outside.

PART 1

Beyond The Noise

The Sacred Power of Slowing Down

He who has a why to live
can bear almost any how.

—Friedrich Nietzsche

If you've been stuck in the glorification of busy, here's a radical idea: ***Give yourself permission to pause.*** *This might feel uncomfortable at first. Our culture doesn't "reward" pausing—there's no prize for taking a break, no raise for work-life balance, no round of applause for saying "I'm taking time for myself." Yet, pausing is essential if you want to trade noise for meaning. When you pause—whether it's taking a single mindful breath in a frantic moment, or actually taking an afternoon off for introspection—you create space for your* ***soul's voice*** *to be heard.*

Giving Yourself Permission to Pause

Remember, *you came here for more than a schedule.* You are more than the sum of your tasks and obligations. In the silence between activities, in the still moments when you're not "useful" to anyone else, you *meet yourself.* You hear the whisper of what your heart really yearns for. It might say, "Hey, I miss being creative," or "I wish we'd spend more time in nature like we used to," or "I'm so tired, can we rest and rethink things?" These gentle inner messages get overpowered when you're racing through life. But when you intentionally slow down, they begin to emerge—and these are golden. They are clues to your unique **celestial calling**—the life that would truly fulfil you, not just look good on paper.

Early in the morning, before the world's demands

flood in, or late at night when the emails stop—those quiet minutes can feel unfamiliar if you usually fill every second. You might feel *fidgety* or even guilty for not doing something "productive." But I challenge you to lean into that discomfort. Try sitting quietly with a journal or just your thoughts. Breathe deeply and ask yourself: *What parts of my life feel like mere busy noise? What activities or commitments no longer resonate with who I truly am?* Listen for the answer. It may come as a clear thought, or maybe an uneasy feeling in your stomach when you think about a certain commitment—a sign that it's not aligned. Conversely, think of times you felt *alive, in the zone*—maybe giving advice to a friend, or playing music, or working on a project that excited you. That warm, expansive feeling in your chest when you recall it? That's a sign of alignment. Your body and emotions are excellent compasses if you give them room to speak.

Reflection Prompt: *If a stranger examined how you spend your time, what would they say matters most to you?* Take a moment to consider if the things consuming your time truly match what you *deeply care about*. You might even list your top 5 life priorities (such as family, creativity, health, spirituality, learning, community, etc.) and then list the top 5 things you spend the most time on. How well do those lists match? This isn't to judge yourself, but to shine a loving light on where life might be out of alignment. Often, simply becoming aware is the first step to change.

Now, you might be wondering: *But I have responsibilities—I can't just drop everything "unfulfiling" and bliss out.* And that's true—we all have duties (jobs, caring for family, etc.) that may not always thrill us. Living with purpose doesn't mean shirking responsibilities or never being busy. It means *approaching even your responsibilities with a new mindset* and making room, wherever possible, for more of what aligns with you. Perhaps you can't change your job overnight, but you can start injecting small moments of alignment into your day—like a short creative practice before work, or meaningful conversation instead of small talk at lunch, or simply being fully present and kind in the tasks you do. And over time, you might start exploring changes that bring your outer life closer to your inner values—maybe a career shift, a schedule adjustment, or setting boundaries to protect non-working time.

Speaking of boundaries, here's a powerful reframe: when you catch yourself saying "I'm too busy to do X," try saying instead "It's not a priority right now." For example, "I'm too busy to exercise" versus "Exercise isn't a priority right now." The latter can feel uncomfortable—and that's the point. It lays bare the choices we're making. If something truly matters, finding even 10 minutes for it is worthwhile. If you genuinely don't have 10 minutes, it might be time to evaluate what's consuming your hours. Sometimes "busy" is just a socially acceptable way to say "*my priorities are elsewhere.*" And that's okay! Your time should be aligned with your priorities. The key is to be **conscious** about it, rather than carried by the inertia of busyness.

3

EMBRACING A LIFE BEYOND THE NOISE

Your time is limited, so don't waste it living someone else's life.

—Steve Jobs

Imagine a life where your **schedule has space***—space for breaths, space for unexpected adventures, space for the people you love and the activities that make you feel alive. In this life, you still get things done, but you do them with intention and presence. You no longer measure your worth by how exhausted you are at day's end. Instead, you gently assess your day by asking: Did I spend it on what matters? Some days the answer will be yes, and you'll feel a deep contentment. Other days, when life's chaos intervenes,* *you'll notice the imbalance and lovingly adjust course for tomorrow.*

Living beyond the noise doesn't mean life is always quiet or slow. It means *you are in tune with the true signal amidst the noise.* You can still have full, active days—but they will be full of what fulfils **you**. You'll start to notice a sense of **flow** replacing that frenzied rushing. Paradoxically, you might accomplish just as much (or even more) toward your dreams when aligned, because you're not wasting energy on aimless busywork or draining commitments. When you engage your heart, not just your head, you tap into an almost supernatural efficiency and creativity. An aligned hour can be more productive than a distracted, busy day.

Soul Prompt—Journal Exercise: *Write down the top three things that you feel "busy" with in life right now.* Then ask for each: "What is my *true* intention in doing this? Is it coming from fear/obligation or love/purpose?" For example, you might write: "I'm busy with volunteering on this committee. True intention? Honestly, fear of saying no and looking selfish." That awareness might lead you to set a boundary or find a way to serve that actually excites you. Or you might write: "I'm busy taking care of my kids. True intention: love—I want to support and nurture them." That's an aligned busy activity (even if tiring, it's rooted in love). This exercise helps distinguish the noise from the music. You can then strategise how to reduce or rework the noisy parts—maybe delegate, simplify, or let go of what's not truly aligned.

As you begin to filter out the noise, something beautiful happens: **peace and clarity return**. You realise that *peace was there all along*, patiently waiting beneath the clamour. With clarity, you become aware of subtle desires or callings that have been trying to get your attention. Perhaps a passion you've shelved for years starts resurfacing. Perhaps a new path or project starts "knocking" on your door through coincidences or persistent ideas (we'll talk more about those signs in Chapter 12). This is the magic of swapping busy for aligned—life actually becomes more *synchronistic* and supportive, because you are finally listening and cooperating with your soul's intentions rather than constantly fighting against the current.

Before we close this chapter, let's ground this in a simple, empowering truth: **You are worthy and enough, even if you slow down.** Your value is not measured by how much you do. You do not have to *earn* your right to rest or to follow your joy. When you were born, nobody handed you a to-do list to prove your worth; you *are* worthy by virtue of being here, of being a living, breathing, feeling soul. Sometimes, we pack our schedules to unconsciously prove we're *good people*, or to avoid feeling guilty. But consider that perhaps the most *responsible* thing you can do for yourself and the world is to **live wholeheartedly**. And that requires listening to your inner compass over the external scorecard of busyness.

Affirmation: *I am more than my to-do list. I give myself permission to slow down and listen. Being busy is not my purpose—being me is my purpose. I choose activities that align with my heart, and I release the rest.*

As you step away from the noise you once mistook for purpose, you'll begin to hear a different voice—a soft, guiding whisper that has been trying to reach you all along. It might ask you to reimagine your path, to dare to do less but live more. Trust that whisper. In the next chapter, we'll talk about those subtle messages—those moments you felt called toward something more but perhaps shrugged it off. For now, celebrate this: by questioning busyness, you've already taken the first step toward alignment. You're tuning your life from static into **music**, from just busy into **truly alive**.

4

YOU HEARD THE WHISPER, DIDN'T YOU?

Follow your bliss and the universe will open doors where there were only walls.

—Joseph Campbell

The Moments You Felt Called but Shrugged It Off

"Life doesn't yell. It whispers."

Have you ever felt something stir inside you during an ordinary moment — a fleeting thought that said, "There's more to life than this"... and then brushed it aside because it didn't fit your schedule?

Maybe it was a conversation that left your heart on fire, a dream that lingered long after you woke up, or a quiet sadness you couldn't explain. Maybe it was a longing to quit your job, change cities, start painting again, or speak up when you usually stay quiet.

You heard the whisper—but you didn't answer.

This chapter is about that whisper.

The one that nudges you at random times. The one that shows up when you're about to settle for something small, whispering, *"Are you sure you're meant for this?"* Most people ignore it. They tell themselves they're being silly, dramatic, unrealistic. But deep down, they know—that whisper came from somewhere important.

Let's stop pretending we didn't hear it.

The Whisper Isn't Loud—It's Sacred

Life rarely slaps us with billboards saying "CHANGE COURSE."

Instead, it gives us nudges. Chills during a line in a movie. A memory that replays in our minds weeks after it "should've" faded. Unexpected emotion when we see someone else living freely. A spontaneous tear when we hear a certain song.

These are not random. They are soul signals.

"The soul doesn't scream. It sends signals."

The more tuned-in we are, the more we catch them. But here's the truth: most people **don't ignore their calling because they don't hear it—they ignore it because they do.**

They hear it.
They just don't think they're ready.

Common Ways We Shrug Off the Whisper

Let's name a few "shrug responses" you may have used when your inner knowing tried to reach you:

1. **"That's just my imagination."** We dismiss inspired ideas because they aren't logical. But imagination is the soul's language.
2. **"I don't have time for this right now."** We treat sacred nudges like optional hobbies instead of invitations to alignment.
3. **"I'm too old / young / busy / unqualified."** The mind gives reasons. The soul gives *readiness.*
4. **"Maybe someday."** Translation: "I'm scared." That's okay. We all are. But "someday" too often becomes never.

If you've ever felt called—then excused it away—this chapter is for you.

The Whisper Is Personal

That whisper you felt? It wasn't meant for your best friend. Or your spouse. Or your co-worker. It was meant **for you.**

You might hear it in a bookstore aisle. Or when journaling. Or while cooking dinner. It might come with goosebumps, or a sudden flash of clarity. It's usually accompanied by a sense of **truth** that words can't explain.

You've heard it before.

Maybe it asked you to leave a toxic relationship.

Maybe it told you to write a book.

Maybe it urged you to rest, to dream again, to say no, or to finally say yes.

Even now, you might remember moments like that—moments when your soul tried to get your attention.

Reflection Prompt

List three moments in your life where you felt something bigger nudging you—but you ignored it. What made you hold back?

The Voice of Ego vs. the Voice of Soul

To follow your celestial calling, you must learn to tell the difference between **ego's fear** and **soul's guidance.**

EGO says:	SOUL says:
"You're not ready."	"You were born for this."
"What will people think?"	"What will you think of yourself if you don't?"

EGO says:	SOUL says:
"Be realistic."	"Be *truthful*."
"Don't risk it."	"This is what you came here to do."

The soul whispers quietly. It doesn't push. It invites.

If the voice in your head is harsh, rushed, or guilt-inducing, it's probably fear. If it feels calm, deep, and strangely familiar—that's your inner compass.

Journaling Cue

When have you felt inner peace, even while contemplating a big, bold decision? Describe that feeling. Where did it come from?

Why We Shrug Off the Sacred

There's a heartbreaking pattern many of us follow:

1. We feel the whisper.
2. We get excited (or terrified).
3. We overthink it.
4. We convince ourselves to stay safe.
5. Life continues… but something feels off.

We do this because we were never taught to **trust our knowing.**

Instead, we were trained to listen to rules, expectations, schedules. We were taught to **justify our dreams** before following them.

But the soul doesn't deal in justification. It deals in *truth.*

And truth often doesn't make sense until you're living it.

What If the Whisper Was Right?

Just for a moment, imagine…

What if the whisper was **right**?

What if that idea wasn't a random thought, but a **download** meant for your path?

What if that longing wasn't a weakness—but a glimpse into your deeper purpose?

What if the emotion you felt was not a "sign of instability," but proof that you're alive and meant for more?

Can you give yourself permission—just for today—to believe the whisper?

Reclaiming the Whisper

The whisper didn't leave. It's been waiting.

Even if you ignored it before, it's not gone. Callings are patient. They're embedded in your very being.

And they don't need you to be perfect—just present.

Soul Statement

"I am not too late. My calling remembers me."

Exercise—The Whisper Map

Create a "whisper map" in your journal:

1. **Divide a page into 3 columns**:
   - *Moment I Felt the Nudge*
   - *What It Whispered*
   - *How I Responded*
2. Look for patterns. Do your whispers involve creativity? Connection? Teaching? Freedom?
3. Reflect: Which whispers are still alive in me? Which ones am I ready to revisit?

Visual Imagery—The Feather and the Flame

Picture this:

A feather floats gently into your hand—light, silent, subtle. That's the whisper. You almost miss it. But it touches something in you. And that light touch, that seemingly weightless moment, can ignite a **flame**—of inspiration, purpose, transformation.

Don't mistake the feather's gentleness for weakness.

The quietest moments often carry the most powerful truth.

Closing Thoughts

You don't have to make a dramatic leap right now.

But you do have to *acknowledge the whisper.* That alone begins the shift.

Once acknowledged, your soul knows you're listening again. And it will begin to speak more clearly.

In the next chapter, we'll look at the false "maps" we've been handed—the timelines we were told to follow. And how unlearning those may be the most liberating thing you'll ever do.

Until then…

Affirmation

I trust the whispers within me. They are not fantasy—they are my compass.

5

THE MAP WAS NEVER LINEAR

The privilege of a lifetime is
to become who you truly are.

—Carl Jung

We're told that life is supposed to unfold in a ***linear*** *fashion.*

Each milestone leads neatly to the next, like steps on a ladder.

Fall in love → Get married → Be happy forever.

Get good grades → Land the job → Live successfully ever after.

Unlearning the Step-by-Step Life Plan

"Some paths are made with footprints, not road signs."

There's a timeline we've all been handed at some point in life.

It usually goes like this:

Go to school.
Get a degree.
Get a job.
Buy a car.
Get married.
Buy a house.
Have kids.
Work hard.
Retire.
Rest.
Die.

There it is.

The "map" that so many are expected to follow—sometimes without ever asking who drew it or whether it leads to the life they truly want.

This chapter is about realizing that **the map you were given might not be yours.**

And that's not a failure—that's freedom.

The Myth of the Straight Path

But that's not how real life works.

In real life, the "job that was supposed to be the

dream" turns out draining.

The "perfect relationship" ends in heartbreak.

The degree collects dust in a career you don't even want anymore.

Here's the truth nobody teaches:

The soul doesn't move in straight lines.

It moves in **spirals**, **zigzags**, and **loops**.

It doubles back. It gets quiet. It makes left turns when you least expect it.

It learns, unlearns, re-learns.

It leads you into detours that become **destinations**.

Reflection Prompt

What life path were you "supposed" to follow? How much of that plan came from your family, culture, or fear—rather than your soul?

When You Realise the Map Doesn't Fit

There's a moment in every person's life when they begin to question the path they're on.

Sometimes it's subtle—a growing sense of restlessness.

Other times, it comes with a jolt—burnout, breakup, breakdown.

This is the moment when your soul whispers:

"You don't have to keep going this way."

The scary part? There might not be a clear alternative path in sight.

You just know the current one feels wrong.

And that's enough. That is sacred information.

"When you realise the road ahead no longer leads to where you want to go, you have every right to turn around."

The Courage to Deviate

Choosing a different path—one that **feels aligned** but doesn't look traditional—requires tremendous courage. Why? Because we fear:

- Disappointing others.
- Looking like a failure.
- Starting over.
- Being misunderstood.

But the real risk isn't deviating.

The real risk is waking up one day and realizing you lived your entire life on someone else's terms.

Remember this:

Deviation isn't destruction. It's redirection.

Just because your journey looks different doesn't mean it's wrong.

In fact, it might be the most sacred thing about you.

Rewriting the Rules

Let's deconstruct a few common timeline myths:

1. **"You should have it all figured out by your 30s."** Truth: Most people are still *figuring it out* well into their 40s, 50s, and beyond.
2. **"You should know what you want to do by 18."** Truth: At 18, you can't legally drink, rent a car, or even understand your own brain chemistry—but somehow you're supposed to choose a lifelong path?
3. **"You're behind."** Truth: Behind *what*? Life isn't a race. There's no referee at the finish line checking if you got married at the "right" age.
4. **"You wasted time."** Truth: Nothing is wasted if it taught you who you are not—and pointed you toward who you truly are.

Soul Statement

"I am allowed to change course. My timeline is not wrong—it's mine."

Signs You're on a Spiral, Not a Straight Line

You might be walking a spiral path if:

- You're returning to a dream you left behind years ago.

- You're trying something you "failed" at before, but this time feels different.
- You keep circling a lesson until you finally get it.
- You feel called to something that doesn't make logical sense but makes your soul expand.

These aren't signs of confusion. They're signs of growth.

Linear maps are for machines.

Spiral maps are for souls.

Real Stories of Nonlinear Becoming

- A woman who left law school to become a yoga teacher.
- A father who started painting at age 52 and sold his first canvas at 60.
- A teen who skipped college and built a global nonprofit from his bedroom.
- A retiree who started a podcast at 70—because her voice finally felt ready.

None of them followed the "standard" path.

All of them answered their **celestial calling**.

Not when it was expected.

But exactly when it was **right**.

Journaling Cue

When have you gone "off script" in your life—and ended up somewhere unexpectedly beautiful?

Throwing Out the Checklist

We are checklist people.

- Married? ✓
- Job with a title? ✓
- Own a home? ✓
- Have kids? ✓

But checklists are a **crude way** to measure a soulful life.

A better checklist might be:

- Have I felt alive this month?
- Did I say yes to something that scared me (in a good way)?
- Have I spent time in awe, wonder, or gratitude?
- Am I becoming more of who I really am?

Those are the metrics of meaning.

Soul Prompt

Create your own "soulful success checklist." What actually matters to you—not just to the world?

6

THE TRUE NATURE OF PURPOSE

To be yourself in a world that is constantly trying to make you something else is the greatest accomplishment.

—Ralph Waldo Emerson

Your purpose isn't just "a thing you do."

It's how you show up in the world.

You could be a teacher today, a traveller tomorrow, a storyteller next year.

But underneath it all, your essence—your reason for being—is expressed in how you live, not just in what you accomplish.

So stop waiting for one perfect path to appear.

Walk *your* path, even if it winds, doubles back, or disappears into fog.

Your feet know the way.

Here's a radical idea:

Purpose isn't a destination. It's a way of being.

Visual Imagery—The River and the Map

Imagine a river trying to follow a printed map.

Every time the map says "go straight," but the landscape curves, the river gets confused.

Eventually, the river stops following the map and starts following the **land**—flowing with grace, trusting the bends, carving beauty into the earth.

You are that river.

The map was never meant to confine you—only to start the journey.

Let life redraw itself through you.

Exercise—Release the Old Timeline

Draw a timeline of your life as you were "told" it should go (what you expected by age 20, 30, 40, etc.).

Next to it, draw another line: your **actual** journey.

Look at where they differ.

Now circle the parts of the *real* path that gave you the most growth, joy, or revelation.

You'll likely discover: the detours were the destination. The messy middle was the magic.

Affirmation

My life is not a line. It is a living dance. I follow my own rhythm and arrive exactly when I'm meant to.

The Map Was Never Linear—Unlearning the Step-by-Step Life Plan

Life is not a straight line, yet many of us were handed a **map** in childhood that showed a single road with neat, sequential stops: school, career, marriage, house, retirement. We were told if we follow this route step-by-step, we'll reach happiness or success right on schedule. But if you've ever felt **lost**, "behind," or as if you took a wrong turn somewhere, take heart. The truth is, **the map was never linear.** Your journey was always meant to be a winding adventure—a divine unfolding with its own perfect timing. In this chapter, we'll explore how to unlearn the rigid life plan you inherited and embrace the beautiful, nonlinear path your soul is actually on.

The Illusion of a Step-by-Step Life Plan

From a young age, many of us absorb the idea that life is a **checklist** of milestones. We learn to measure progress by how closely we stick to this script. Consider some of the typical items on the "life plan" checklist:

- **Education by a Certain Age:** *Graduate high school by 18, college by 22.*
- **Career Launch:** *Secure a stable job right after graduation.*
- **Family and Marriage:** *Find a lifelong partner, marry by 30, have children by a planned timeline.*
- **Homeownership and Stability:** *Buy a house, settle into a long-term career, climb the ladder.*
- **Retirement Plan:** *Work steadily until 65, then retire to enjoy the fruits of labor.*

On paper, it sounds tidy. There's comfort in thinking life can be approached like a scheduled program—no surprises, no lost time. **But life often has other plans.** You might finish school **later** than expected or skip college altogether. You might change careers in midlife or decide not to marry, or you could face unexpected events like illness, layoffs, or moves that **completely redraw your map**. When reality doesn't match the tidy checklist, it's easy to feel like you've failed or fallen off track.

We equate our worth with adhering to the plan, thinking that if we just check all the boxes on time, we'll be okay. Society, family, or culture might have ingrained in us that deviating from the timeline means something is wrong. If you're single at 35 when everyone expected you married, or exploring a new career at 40 when others have been in one field for decades, you may feel "*behind*." But this feeling comes from comparing yourself to an

illusion—a one-size-fits-all timeline that never accounted for your soul's individuality.

Unlearning the step-by-step life plan begins with recognising it *was an inherited script, not a divine decree.* Who wrote that script for you? Perhaps well-meaning parents, teachers, or the surrounding culture wrote it based on what they knew. But **your life is not a script to perform; it's an experience to live.** There is no universal schedule that every person must follow to live a meaningful life. The "straight path" is a mirage. Real journeys zigzag, loop back, and take detours. And that's *not only okay—it's often where the magic happens.*

PART 2

DIVINE TIMING VS. HUMAN TIMELINES

ART OF PURPOSE, EMOTION, AND ACTION

You must find the place
inside yourself where
nothing is impossible.

—Deepak Chopra

One of the core metaphysical ideas that helps us break free from the linear life script is divine timing. Divine timing is the belief that events unfold in our lives at the right moment, guided by a higher wisdom or the flow of the Universe. It suggests that we are not "late"—we're right on time for our unique journey. While human timelines are all about deadlines ("I should do X by age Y"), divine timing invites us to loosen our grip on when things should happen.

Think of how nature operates. A sunflower sprouts, blooms, and seeds in its own season. It would be absurd for the sunflower to compare itself to the rose blooming earlier in spring. In the same way, **your soul has its own season for blooming**. You might land your dream career at 50, or find your true love after a divorce, or discover a passion for painting in your sixties. None of these are "wrong" or "late"—they're perfectly timed for the unfolding of **your purpose**.

Yet, when life doesn't match the timeline we expected, we often panic. We ask, "*Why hasn't it happened for me yet? What am I doing wrong?*" It's easy to internalise shame or anxiety, feeling you need to play **catch-up** with everyone else. If you've been feeling this way, here's a gentle reminder: **there is no race and no finish line** in the soul's journey. We are all on different paths entirely. The concept of being "behind" is a myth, a product of comparing incomparable lives.

Journal Prompt: *Whose timeline are you following?* Take a moment to reflect in writing: List some life milestones you feel pressured about (e.g., "I thought I'd have ___ by now."). Next to each, write down where that expectation came from. Was it a family expectation? A cultural norm? A story of a friend's life? Seeing the source can help you realise these timelines are *not* universal truths—they're borrowed expectations you have the power to release.

Trusting the Unfolding

Embracing divine timing means **trusting the unfolding** of events, even when you can't foresee where they lead. It's like walking through fog with only a lantern—you might only see a few steps ahead, but that's enough. You trust that as you move, more of the path will be revealed. This trust can feel radical in a world that values planning and control. It requires a shift from *"I'm late"* to *"I'm exactly where I need to be right now."*

Let's consider an example of how divine timing can play out. **Ari's story** comes to mind:

Ari was a talented graphic designer who always assumed she'd have a thriving career by 25. She watched classmates land big jobs right after college, while she struggled to find steady work. At 26, feeling panicked, she took a job in an unrelated field just to pay bills, telling herself she had fallen behind. But that "detour" introduced her to a whole new industry and mentor. Two years later, through that mentor, she was offered an amazing design role at a company that truly valued her art style. In hindsight, the timing was perfect—at 25 she wasn't ready and the job she eventually got didn't even exist yet! Ari realised that what felt like a delay was actually ***divine coordination****: the right opportunity and her readiness happened together. If she'd forced the timeline earlier, she might have ended up in a job that wasn't a fit.*

Ari's experience illustrates the power of trusting that **life's delays are not denials**—often, they're preparing you for something better or aligning circumstances in ways you can't see yet. She went from feeling "late" to understanding she was right on time for *her* path.

In moments when you worry that you're off schedule, try this **affirmation**: *I release the need to follow anyone else's timeline. I am on* ***soul time****, and I am exactly where I need to be.* Repeat it to yourself whenever anxiety about "being behind" creeps in. Over time, you'll start to internalise a new belief that **your life isn't off track at all**—it's unfolding in its own beautiful order.

The Soul's Spiral Path—Growth Is Not Linear

While we often speak of the "path of life," it's important to remember that it's *not a straight highway* from point

A to B. Many wisdom traditions say that **life moves in a spiral or cycles** rather than a line. You may notice you return to similar themes or challenges over the years, each time with a new understanding. This is the **soul's spiral path**: we grow outward and upward, but we circle back to deepen our learning.

Picture a **spiral staircase**: you go round and round, and it might feel like you're near where you started, but you've actually ascended to a higher floor. Likewise, you might find yourself revisiting an old dream or an old obstacle after many years. This doesn't mean you've gone backwards—it means you're seeing it from a higher vantage now, with more wisdom than before. **Life will revisit lessons** until we fully grasp them, and that's part of our evolution, not a mistake.

For example, perhaps in your early twenties you struggled with self-worth at work, believing you had to prove yourself. Decades later, you might confront self-worth again after a layoff or a career change. It can feel like, "*Oh no, I'm back where I started.*" But in truth, you have years of experience behind you this time. You're able to approach the situation with more resilience and insight. **The context has changed, and so have you.** The issue circles back not to torment you, but to allow you to resolve it at a deeper level—to finally affirm your worth from within. This spiral of returning themes is how the soul gently pushes us toward growth and authenticity.

Embracing Identity Evolution

Just as our journey isn't linear, **who we are is not fixed either**. We often latch onto an identity—"I am a teacher," "I am a shy person," "I am the responsible eldest child who must do XYZ"—and we build a life plan around that static identity. But over time, experiences stretch and transform us. You're allowed to evolve and even *change fundamentally* as you follow your spiral path.

One year you might identify strongly with being a world-traveling free spirit; another season of life you crave putting down roots and being a homebody. Neither is the "real" you—or rather, *both* are. Your identity can be multifaceted and changeable. Unlearning the step-by-step plan involves **letting go of the notion that you must be one thing all your life.** You came here to be **many things, to wear many costumes of the soul**, in different chapters of your story.

Unlearning the "One Path" Mindset

If you have been rigidly holding onto *one* identity or *one* life plan, try to loosen that grip. **Unlearning the linear mindset** means opening up to the idea that there are many paths you could walk and many selves you could be—and *all* would enrich your soul. Instead of asking, "Am I on the **right path**?" consider that *life has many* *right paths.* The question to ask is, "Does this path **feel true** to me right now?" If yes, walk it. If it later feels false or constraining, you can change direction.

One practical tool here is to reflect on **core values and feelings** rather than rigid goals. Perhaps your core values are creativity, freedom, and service. There are dozens of careers or lifestyles through which you could honour those values—not just the one you first imagined. If your original plan doesn't let you live your core values, it's not a failure to pivot; it's wisdom.

Reflection Exercise: *Write down 3-5 core values or experiences that matter most to you (e.g., freedom, family, learning, adventure, helping others, spirituality). Then write a few ways you could express each of those in your life.* This exercise shows you that there isn't a single route to fulfilment. There are countless ways to live out what's most important to you. Realizing this helps loosen the fear that you must stick to one narrow track or else miss your chance at a meaningful life.

7

PERSONAL DETOURS: TURNING "OFF TRACK" INTO OPPORTUNITY

You cannot always control what goes on outside.
But you can always control what goes on inside.

—Wayne Dyer

Sometimes the best way to internalise these lessons is through stories. Let's explore a few real-life detours and the unexpected gifts they carried. These anecdotes (names changed for privacy) illustrate that what feels like being "off track" can actually be the route to your truest life.

1. When a Dream Job Becomes a Dead-End: *Marisol* had her life mapped out from day one of college. She pursued pharmacy, a field she was told was secure and respected. She did everything "right"—top grades, the right internships—and landed a job at a big hospital by 24. By 27, however, Marisol felt strangely empty. She was successful by all external measures, but each morning she dreaded going to work. *"What's wrong with me?"* she thought. *"I have what I planned for. Why am I unhappy?"*

It took a health scare in her family—her mother's diagnosis of diabetes—to shake Marisol awake. As she helped her mother through lifestyle changes, Marisol discovered she was deeply passionate about **holistic nutrition and wellness**. She found herself spending free time researching herbal remedies and coaching her mom through diet changes. This was a far cry from the stable pharmacy career she had planned. Eventually, Marisol made the courageous choice to go back to school for a degree in nutrition and public health. Many people in her life were baffled—*"You're starting over?"* they asked. But for Marisol, it felt less like starting over and more like **coming home to herself**. Now in her mid-30s, she runs a wellness practice and says she feels *alive* every day, in a way she never did following the step-by-step plan. Her pharmacy background even helps her in a niche she couldn't see when she started. What seemed like a detour or a "dead-end" job was actually the Universe nudging Marisol toward a more fulfiling calling.

Lesson: Sometimes achieving a goal can reveal that it wasn't what your soul truly wanted. Don't be afraid to course-correct when an unexpected passion takes hold of you. The courage to pivot can lead you to work that **lights you up**, even if it diverges from your original roadmap.

2. The Relationship That Redefined Success: *Dev* prided himself on being a high achiever, and that included his personal life. He had a picture in his head of the "ideal timeline"—meet the perfect partner by 28, marry by 30, kids by 32. He was on track, engaged to his college sweetheart, working a well-paying job, checking all the boxes. Then life threw a curveball: at 29, just months before the wedding, his fiancée called it off. She tearfully admitted she wasn't ready and felt they were growing in different directions. Dev was blindsided and heartbroken. In his mind, this was not only a personal loss but a **failure to stay on schedule**. All his friends were getting married; he felt like the odd one out, the one who "couldn't make it work."

In the aftermath, Dev went through a dark night of the soul. Without the relationship that had anchored his future plans, he started questioning everything. Was the corporate job he rushed to get making him happy? If he had kids, what wisdom would he even pass on to them about life? With time and the help of a good therapist, Dev started seeing the breakup as an invitation to know himself beyond the roles of husband or father that he'd been so fixated on. He took a year to travel solo—something he never would have done otherwise—and on a volunteer trip building homes, he met people who lived very differently, valuing community and presence over achievement. It completely shifted his perspective.

Today, Dev is in a new relationship, but he approaches love and success with a *whole new mindset*. He no longer views marriage or a certain salary as the markers of having "made it." Instead, he defines success as **being true to himself and present in each moment**. Ironically, once he let go of the rigid timeline, life flowed more easily. He met his current partner casually through a shared hobby (when he wasn't "looking"), and their connection is far more aligned with his authentic self. Dev often says that breaking off the planned path—as painful as it was—**set him free** to find a version of happiness that's actually his own, not what he thought it should be.

Lesson: A major personal detour like a breakup or divorce can feel like a derailment of your life plan. But it might redirect you to *find yourself*. It can teach you that your worth is not defined by your relationship status or how closely you meet societal expectations. **Sometimes a "wrong turn" in love brings you to the right relationship—starting with the relationship with yourself.**

3. Awakening Through Adversity: *Sasha's* journey took an unexpected turn through a health crisis. A driven entrepreneur, Sasha was used to planning everything—

from five-year business growth targets to meticulously scheduled days. Her identity was wrapped up in being *productive* and always ahead of the curve. But in her early 40s, Sasha was diagnosed with a serious autoimmune illness. Suddenly, she couldn't work 60-hour weeks; some days, just getting out of bed was a victory. This event shattered her step-by-step life plan in one swift blow. She had to pause her business and focus on healing, an unplanned "stop" that filled her with fear. *"I'm losing time, I'm falling behind,"* she worried as months went by.

Yet in the forced stillness and uncertainty, Sasha experienced a profound inner awakening. With her usual busy routine stripped away, she began **exploring spiritual practices**—first as a way to cope with anxiety about her illness. She started meditating and journaling, delving into questions of purpose beyond work. In the quiet hours of reflection, Sasha realised how numb she had become by rushing through life. She had been so focused on the next goal that she rarely savoured the present. As her body slowly healed, her spirit was reborn. She describes this period as *"walking through a fog and finding a new sunrise on the other side."* Eventually, Sasha returned to her business but in a completely different style—with balance and compassion for herself, and a new venture mentoring others on wellness and mindset. What she thought was the end of her productive life turned into the **beginning of a more meaningful chapter**.

Lesson: An unexpected challenge or hardship can awaken parts of your soul that success and smooth sailing never could. When life makes you slow down or takes you on an unplanned pause, it might be a sacred detour. Within the pain or uncertainty, there may lie an opportunity to discover deeper resilience, new passions (like Sasha's spiritual interests), and a more authentic way of living. **Your soul's path sometimes includes traversing the dark to discover your inner light.**

These stories underline a common truth: **what looks like a detour is often the real path**. When things don't go according to plan, it's not because you did something wrong—it might be because there's something more for you to learn or experience. Each of these individuals eventually felt gratitude for the very experiences that once made them feel lost. You too may one day look back on your current detour and see how it brought you **exactly where you needed to be**.

8

PRACTICAL TOOLS FOR EMBRACING AN UNCONVENTIONAL PATH

Remember that wherever your heart is,
there you will find your treasure.

—Paulo Coelho

Breaking away from the linear life plan isn't just a one-time decision—it's an ongoing practice. Here are some ***practical tools and habits*** *to support you as you navigate a non-traditional, more fluid life journey:*

- **Mindfulness and Presence:** When you feel anxious about the future or compare yourself to others, bring your attention to the **present moment**. Practices like meditation or simply a few deep breaths can ground it when new information or opportunities come. One practical approach is the "pivot plan": when you set a goal, also jot down a plan B or C that you'd be okay exploring if Plan A doesn't pan out. This keeps your mind open to life's surprises. Remember, **an open mind sees alternatives; a rigid mind sees failure when plans change**.

- **Celebrate Milestones Differently:** In the step-by-step life plan, only big milestones count (graduation, wedding, promotion, etc.). On the nonlinear journey, *every step forward, every lesson learned is a milestone.* Get in the habit of celebrating your **inner milestones**. Did you overcome a fear? That's huge! Did you follow your intuition on a tough decision even though others doubted you? Bravo! Maybe you finally set a boundary or gave yourself permission to try something new—these are all victories on the unconventional path. You might keep a "joy journal" or monthly reflection to list things you're proud of that wouldn't make a traditional resume but absolutely enrich your life story.

Using these tools, you build a kind of **navigation system for your soul's journey**. You learn to steer by inner wisdom and adaptability, rather than by fixed routes. Yes, there will still be uncertainty—that's part of being alive—but you'll be better equipped to handle it. Instead of fearing the unknown, you can start to see it as an adventure and an ally.

time, your journal becomes a map of its own-
that charts your inner growth rather than ext
milestones. Re-reading old entries can show you
far you've come in perspectives and highlight pat
or passions that keep emerging, which is guic
from your inner self on what to pursue next.

Mentors and Models: Seek out stories and peopl
inspire you to embrace unconventional paths. It
be a friend who changed careers at 50, or a p
figure who took a non-traditional route to su
Hearing others' experiences can normalise your
If possible, talk to mentors or join communities
online groups) of people who prioritise purp
living over following the crowd. **Surrounding yo
with diverse narratives** makes it easier to reme
that there's no single "right" way. It also provides su
for those days you doubt yourself—you can reca
examples of people who thrived by trusting their

Flexible Planning: It's not that you must aband
plans—it's about **planning with flexibility** and
Set intentions rather than rigid goals. For exa
instead of "I must become a manager by next
you might set an intention like "I will grov
leadership skills and seek opportunities to lead."
focuses on your *growth* and *values* rather than
by a deadline. By all means, map out steps towarc
dreams, but hold the map lightly. Be willing to

you. Mindfulness reminds you that life is happening *now*, not in a hypothetical future. It helps you trade obsession over timelines for appreciation of what *is*. Even a short daily practice—for example, a morning five-minute meditation focusing on the mantra *"I am exactly where I'm meant to be right now"*—can re-centre your mind toward trust.

- **Affirmations and Soul Statements:** Words carry power. Consistently repeating positive statements can help rewire your beliefs. Try writing affirmations on sticky notes or in your phone and reviewing them each day. Some examples: *"I measure my life in meaning, not in milestones." "I allow my path to unfold naturally." "Every season of my life serves my growth."* Find phrasing that resonates deeply with you. You can also create a longer **"soul statement"**—a few sentences about what you believe and intend for your journey. For instance: *"I am a soul on a unique journey. I trust the timing of my life and the wisdom of my detours. I choose to live by inspiration, not obligation."* Reading or speaking such statements regularly fortifies your mindset against outside pressures.
- **Journaling for Clarity:** As noted earlier, journaling is a powerful tool for self-discovery. When you feel lost or uncertain, **write it out**. You don't have to have a prompt; just doing a "brain dump" of your worries and hopes can bring relief and insight. Over

9

CRACKS IN THE ROUTINE—WHEN BURNOUT, BOREDOM, AND BREAKDOWN ARE ACTUALLY BREAKTHROUGHS

Trust yourself. You know more than you think you do.

—Benjamin Spock

What if your burnout or breakdown isn't an ending, but a beginning? It's a daring question to ask when you're exhausted, numb, or feeling like everything is falling apart. But countless souls have discovered that the moments when life cracks open—when burnout, boredom, or breakdown strike—are often the first steps of a profound transformation. As media theorist Marshall McLuhan once observed, "every breakdown is a breakthrough". The very fractures in our routine that cause us pain may also let the light in, illuminating a new path forward.

Most of us know too well the slow drip of burnout or the dull ache of a stagnant routine. Modern burnout can arrive quietly—*"the slow, creeping numbness that [comes] from doing too much, feeling too little, and never really stopping"*. It often doesn't *scream* so much as **whisper**, until one day you wake up and realise you've forgotten what it feels like to be truly alive. Boredom, too, can settle like a fog over the heart—that sense that you're merely going through the motions, each day a carbon copy of the last, your spirit wilting from lack of inspiration. If you've felt these things, you're far from alone. Burnout has become so prevalent that the World Health Organization now defines it as a syndrome from chronic workplace stress, marked by exhaustion, cynicism, and reduced effectiveness. And researchers suggest that even **boredom** serves a purpose: it's a functional emotion that *"encourages the pursuit of alternative goals and experiences"* when our current life is no longer satisfying. In other words, your weariness and restlessness are **signals**—messages from your soul and psyche that something needs to change.

Yet in the thick of it, burnout or breakdown can feel like failure. You might think, *"Why can't I handle this? Why am I so drained by what others seem to manage?"* But here's a gentle reframe: **what if your distress is not**

a weakness, but a sign of your soul's wisdom? What if feeling empty at work or overwhelmed by life is your deeper self telling you that you've outgrown your old patterns? The **fatigue of the soul** is real—a kind of tiredness no amount of sleep can fix—and it often points to "sacred redirection." Rather than seeing burnout or emotional collapse as a breakdown of *you*, consider that it might be a breakdown of the *false or limited life* you've been living. The cracks in your routine appear when **your spirit is trying to break free**. In those cracks, as painful as they are, something new is trying to emerge.

The Breaking Point as a Hidden Beginning

Let's look at how a breaking point can secretly become a turning point. Sometimes the stories of others can illuminate our own path. Consider **Lynn's story**: After decades in a high-pressure corporate HR career, Lynn hit a wall of burnout. She felt empty and ill, as if her life-force had been drained by years of nonstop schedules and corporate politics. In the depths of her breakdown, she began exploring the art and spirituality that had always called to her quietly. Over time, Lynn left the corporate grind entirely and followed an unlikely passion—working with sacred geometry and intuitive art—transforming her career into something that fed her soul. What began as a collapse in an HR office became a **breakthrough into a creative, spiritually fulfiling life**. Her burnout was not the end of her success; it was the **dawn of her true calling**.

Lynn's experience is just one example. In another personal account, an entrepreneur described **hitting rock bottom** during a dark winter of stress and depression, utterly burned out from chasing business goals. At first, he felt detached from life, drained of purpose. But at that lowest point, he made a crucial choice: instead of running away or trying to numb the pain, he **surrendered** to it. He allowed himself to feel and to ask what the pain was trying to tell him. In doing so, he "discovered a commitment to surrender and emerged transformed" with a renewed sense of purpose and heart. He stepped back, re-evaluated what truly mattered to him, and redesigned his work and life in a healthier, more meaningful way. His breakdown became a **breakthrough**—the very crisis that forced him to change also freed him to find his light and **his purpose**.

Take a moment to think about that pattern: **struggle—surrender—breakthrough**. We see it over and over, in big lives and "ordinary" lives alike. A high-powered attorney burns out, takes a sabbatical, and realises she wants to start an NGO that aligns with her values. A student overwhelmed by anxiety drops out for a semester, then has an epiphany about a different field of study that truly ignites his passion. A single parent hits exhaustion and despair, asks for help for the first time, and discovers a community of support that changes everything. In each case, **the moment of cracking** led to truth and renewal. The **ending** of one way of life became the **beginning** of a richer one.

It's not that pain magically equals growth—it's that pain *invites* us to grow if we listen. Your **breaking point** may feel like being stuck in a dark tunnel, but it can actually be a passageway. **"When Jove had a migraine, it turned out to be Minerva,"** McLuhan quipped—a metaphor meaning that a splitting headache gave birth to a goddess of wisdom. Our own headaches and heartaches can birth new wisdom in us. The **breakdown** forces a break *with* the past and with habits that no longer serve us. It demands we find a new route—a breakthrough we might never have sought without a push.

Soul Fatigue and Sacred Redirection

Why do these breaking points happen? On a metaphysical level, you could say it's your **soul trying to get your attention**. When you live too long in a way that stifles your spirit—whether it's an unfulfiling job, an inauthentic relationship, or simply a life too small for who you really are—you begin to suffer "soul fatigue." One writer described it perfectly: *"It's not just the body that gives up. It's the soul."* You become *soul-tired*, a weariness that goes beyond physical exhaustion. It's as if your very essence is saying, *"Enough. I can't continue like this."* This kind of deep fatigue is a red flag that something in your life is out of alignment with your **true self**.

Often, before a big change, life will throw hints of this misalignment. You might find yourself chronically bored—a sign that you're not engaged with what makes you feel alive. Or you experience growing irritability, anxiety, or sadness that you can't quite explain. You might succeed on the surface, yet feel empty inside. These are the **whispers of the soul**. If we ignore the whispers, they get louder. **Burnout** is one way the soul shouts, "Stop! Pay attention!" It's a forcing mechanism, slowing you down by draining your energy, effectively pushing you to question everything. In spiritual terms, this is often a **call to awaken**. The parts of you that have been denied or suppressed are demanding acknowledgement.

Think of it as the universe gently (or not so gently) redirecting your course. Sometimes what feels like a loss—a job ending, a relationship breaking down, a door closing—is actually **sacred redirection**. A chapter needs to end so a new one can begin. A routine that once felt stable may now feel confining because *you have grown*. Your soul is ready for an upgrade, and the old routines can't contain the new expansion. It's as if life says, *"You're meant for more than this familiar pattern."* The breakdown removes the lesser so you can make room for the greater.

Seen this way, **burnout is not a failure of yours**—it's evidence of your inner wisdom. Only **engaged, caring people get burnout**; if you didn't care at all, you'd just be apathetic. Burnout often hits those who pushed themselves hard or poured their heart into what they thought they needed to do. It's a sign that your **effort and energy need a new direction**, one more aligned with your heart. Similarly, boredom isn't laziness; it's an alarm that you're **under-living your life**, that you need more meaning, creativity, or challenge. And a breakdown—whether emotional or physical—often serves to break down the ego's agenda and open you to the soul's agenda.

Many spiritual traditions talk about this in different words. In the hero's journey, the hero must fall into the "abyss" or endure a dark night before they can be reborn with new insight. In mystical terms, the "**dark night of the soul**" (a concept from St. John of the Cross) is a period of intense hardship and doubt that precedes spiritual illumination. It's as if **the soul takes us into darkness to find our deeper light**. Your own dark night might be a period of depression, a severe burnout, or a personal crisis. It is *awful* to go through—no sugarcoating that. But it helps to remember, when you are in it, that this darkness is not permanent and not purposeless. It is a **fertile darkness**, in which new life is preparing to germinate.

If you are in that space now, honour it. As uncomfortable as it is, try not to just push it away. **Listen** to what your discomfort is telling you. You might journal about it (some prompts are coming below) or simply sit quietly and feel where the pain is in your body, where the emptiness resides. Ask inwardly, "*What part of me have I been neglecting? What is my heart longing for that I have denied?*" The answers may not come all at once, but simply posing the questions starts a shift. You begin to align with the idea that *this burnout or breakdown is happening for me, not just to me*. It's a turning point.

When you can embrace that perspective—even a tiny bit—you reclaim your power from the situation. Rather than seeing yourself as a victim of overwork or bad luck, you become the hero on a transformational journey. This doesn't mean you wished for the pain, but you recognise your soul's fingerprints on the process. **Life is guiding you**. The **universe** (or God, or whatever guiding force you believe in) might be closing one path so you will take the one you're truly meant to travel. A rejection becomes redirection. A breakdown becomes a breakthrough. That shift in mindset is profoundly liberating. As one inspirational saying goes, "*What if this isn't a breakdown at all, but a breakthrough in disguise?*"—a chance to rebuild your life on a stronger, truer foundation.

Nature's Reminders: Seeds, Cocoons, and Cracks

A green plant sprouting through a crack in concrete, symbolizing resilience and new life emerging from hardened structures. The natural world is full of **visual metaphors** for this process of breakdown-to-breakthrough. Think of a tiny seed sprouting: the seed's shell actually **splits open** in order for the seedling to emerge. If you didn't know better, you might think the seed was destroyed—cracked and broken. But in truth, the *breaking* of the seed coat is what allows the plant to grow. Similarly, the rigid routines and identities we build can become like a shell around us. When life cracks that shell—through a big change or collapse—it can feel like we're breaking apart. In reality, that crack may be exactly how **our new self can break through**. It's fitting to recall songwriter Leonard Cohen's famous lyric: *"There is a crack in everything... that's how the light gets in."*. The **light of insight, hope, and change** often reaches us through the cracks of our broken expectations. We try so hard to be perfect and hold it all together, but the **perfect offering** isn't what life wants from us. Life wants us—the real us, cracks and all, shining our light.

Have you ever seen a plant grow through asphalt or between the bricks of a wall? It's a stunning image of nature's determination. Our souls have that same determination to **live and grow**, even in tough circumstances. When you feel something inside you pushing against the "concrete" of a stuck situation—that's your inner life finding a way. The concrete might be a stifling job or a toxic relationship or a way of living that no longer nourishes you. At first, you notice hairline fractures: you start to admit *"I can't do this anymore"* or *"I'm not happy"*. Those are the initial cracks. Then perhaps something dramatic happens—you get sick, or you have a panic attack, or you receive hard news—and the crack widens. It can be scary, like a dam breaking. But once the water of truth starts flowing, **new energy pours through**. The old structure (the dam, the pavement, the routine) can't hold back your soul's need for change.

A monarch butterfly in its cocoon (chrysalis) stage—a powerful metaphor for the transformative "cocoon" period of breakdown before breakthrough. One of the most beautiful metaphors for personal transformation is the **caterpillar's metamorphosis**. Inside the cocoon, the caterpillar literally dissolves into an unformed goo. If you judged the process midway, you'd think the creature was utterly destroyed. It's a kind of biological **breakdown**—the old form disintegrates. But from that apparent mess emerges a completely new being: the butterfly. Importantly, the butterfly doesn't *step out* of the cocoon unchanged—it **struggles** its way out. The effort of breaking out of the chrysalis strengthens its wings so it can fly. If someone tried to "helpfully" cut the cocoon open early, the butterfly would be too weak to survive. It needs the **struggle** to build its power.

Think of this when you feel like you're in the darkest, most formless stage of change—your own **cocoon stage**. You might say, *"I have no idea who I am anymore, everything's fallen apart."* That is the moment to have faith that **a new form is evolving**. Your job is to keep going, to gently struggle through—seek insight here, practice self-care there, reach out for support when you need it. This is how you strengthen your wings. Your breakdown is forging a breakthrough, but you have to participate in the process. It's *hard*, no doubt about it. The caterpillar probably isn't having a fun time in there either! But it's a sacred process. On the other side of it, you may hardly recognise the **beautiful life** that's born from your willingness to grow.

Reflection: Where Is Your Routine Crushing Your Spirit?

It's time to turn inward and reflect on your own life. Grab a journal or simply ponder these questions. They're designed to help you identify the **cracks in your routine**—those places where your spirit feels crushed or constrained. Write freely and honestly; this is just for you. Often, awareness is the first step toward change.

- **Energy Audit:** What parts of your daily routine drain you the most? List any activities, responsibilities, or habits that leave you feeling exhausted or numb. Why do you think they have this effect?
- **Moments of Dread:** Is there a point in your day or week that you *consistently* dread or feel anxious about? Describe what it is and what you feel in those moments. What would you rather be doing or feeling instead?
- **Autopilot vs. Alive:** Where in your life are you just "going through the motions"? Contrast that with moments you've felt truly **alive**, engaged, or joyful in the past. What were you doing, and what does that tell you about what your soul loves?
- **Values Check:** Write down your top 3 personal values or things that matter most to you (e.g. creativity, family, adventure, service, spirituality, learning, etc.). Now ask: does your current routine honour these values? Where is there a gap between what you care about and how you spend your time?
- **Inner Voice:** If your deep self or soul could speak without censorship, what would it say about your current lifestyle? You might even try writing a letter from your soul to you, starting with "Dear ____, I have been trying to tell you…" and see what pours out.
- **The Breaking Point:** Honestly reflect on this: *Are you close to a breaking point?* What signs of burnout,

boredom, or even breakdown have you been noticing in yourself? List them out. Sometimes seeing it on paper clarifies that *yes, something is cracking.* How might this "breaking" actually be "breaking **through**" to a new chapter for you?

Take your time with these prompts—you might spread them over several days of journaling. The goal is to shine a gentle light on the sore spots in your routine and life. These are the areas ripe for transformation. **Awareness** can in itself be healing. As you identify the cracks, you may feel grief or anger or fear; that's normal. Let those feelings flow. They've been trying to get your attention. By listening now, you're already beginning the process of change.

Soul Statements and Affirmations for Transformation

When you're navigating discomfort and uncertainty, it helps to have a few **affirmations**—or as we might call them here, **soul statements**—to anchor you. These are positive, empowering thoughts you can repeat to yourself. They serve as reminders of the bigger picture when you're caught in day-to-day stress. Choose any that resonate, or write your own. Speak them aloud in the morning or before bed, or anytime you need a boost. Even if at first you only half-believe the words, keep repeating them; over time, they sink in and start to shift your mindset.

- I honour these cracks in my life, for they are openings for light to enter.
- My worth is not defined by my productivity or perfection. I am enough as I am, even in this pause.
- I trust that this challenge is guiding me to grow in ways I can't fully see yet.
- I am allowed to change course. It's safe for me to let go of what no longer feels right.
- My feelings of burnout and boredom are messages, not permanent conditions. I listen to them and respond with love.
- I embrace the discomfort as a catalyst for my transformation. I won't break—I'm breaking through.
- I am rediscovering what makes my soul come alive, and I give myself permission to pursue it.
- Every day, I become more aligned with my true path. Small steps are still progress.
- I deserve rest and renewal. By caring for myself, I am preparing for my breakthrough.
- I invite divine guidance (or intuition) to show me the way forward. I am open to miracles of change.

Feel free to modify the wording to fit your beliefs (for example, use "*I am guided by the universe*" or "*I trust my inner wisdom*"—whatever feels powerful to you). You might post your favourite affirmation on your mirror or as a note in your workspace. The key is to remind yourself that **you have the strength and the permission to evolve**. You're not stuck; you're in process. And you came here—to this earth, this life—for more than just grinding through days. You have a **celestial calling**, a purpose that lights you up. These affirmations reinforce that truth, especially in moments when you doubt or feel lost.

Tools for Turning Pain into Power

Breakthroughs don't happen only by epiphany; they also come through intentional action. Here are some practical tools and steps to help you **navigate burnout** and use your emotional pain as an **invitation to change**. Think of these as ways to support yourself as you transform discomfort into growth. You don't have to do everything at once—even one or two small steps can start building momentum:

1. **Simplify and Release:** When you're burned out or overwhelmed, the first step is often to **clear some space**. Look at your commitments and see what can be trimmed. Like a gardener pruning dead branches, you may need to say no, delegate, or drop tasks that aren't essential. This isn't quitting; it's creating room to heal and reevaluate. Even tiny changes—cancelling a non-critical meeting, pausing a volunteer duty,

putting a project on hold—can relieve pressure and signal to your psyche that it's okay to put yourself first. *Your life upgrade might begin with subtraction.* Release something that feels like a heavy weight.

2. **Prioritise Self-Care Basics:** It sounds obvious, but under stress we forget the fundamentals: **sleep, nutrition, movement, and hydration**. Chronic exhaustion or stress can literally impair our ability to see possibilities. Aim to get more restful sleep (even if it means going to bed earlier or napping), and fuel your body with nourishing food instead of caffeine/sugar rollercoasters. Gentle exercise—a walk in nature, yoga, dancing in your living room—can help discharge stress and clear the mind. Research shows exercise in particular can help prevent and reverse burnout. Think of these habits not as chores, but as **acts of love for your future self**. When you care for your body, you strengthen the vessel that carries your soul. This gives you a sturdier foundation for any life changes you'll make.
3. **Build an Identity Outside the "Old Routine":** One reason burnout hits so hard is that we sometimes tie up our identity in the very roles that are wearing us down (e.g. being the "dependable worker" or "supermom" or "the one who always holds it together"). To break this cycle, **explore parts of yourself beyond those roles**. Rekindle hobbies or interests that you shelved.

Try something new that you've always been curious about—take a photography class, join a weekend hiking group, learn to play an instrument, anything that sounds fun or meaningful. This isn't "escaping" real life; it's expanding it. As you invest time in activities that *fill your cup*, your sense of self widens. You'll find that you are creative, or adventurous, or spiritual, or whatever, beyond what your resume or daily routine says. This not only brings joy back into your days, it also provides clues toward what changes you want in your bigger picture.

4. **Have Honest Conversations and Set Boundaries:** If your routine is crushing you, chances are there are people in your life who need to know. This might be your boss, your partner, your family, or others who rely on you. It can be hard to speak up—especially if you're used to being the rock for everyone—but **honest communication is often necessary for change**. Tell your manager you're overwhelmed and discuss ways to adjust your workload or role (they may surprisingly understand, especially in today's awareness of burnout). Talk to your family about sharing responsibilities or giving you some personal time. Setting boundaries might mean telling others "I don't have the capacity for X right now," and also telling *yourself* that it's okay to not be available for everyone 24/7. Remember the tip: say "I **don't** do

that" instead of "I **can't**," to make the boundary clear and firm. For example, "I don't work past 7 PM anymore" or "I don't check emails on Sundays." These boundaries protect the space you need to recuperate and reinvent yourself.

5. **Seek Support and Don't Go It Alone: Isolation** makes burnout and breakdown far worse. There's immense power in sharing what you're going through with someone you trust. Reach out to a friend, a family member, a support group, or a mentor. Sometimes just verbalizing "I'm really struggling" lifts a weight. You might be amazed how many people respond with "I've been there too" or offer help. If you feel your usual circle doesn't understand, consider a **therapist or coach**. A professional can provide a safe space to unpack your feelings and give you structured tools to cope. Therapy isn't just for when things are *terrible*; it's also for when you sense you need a change and want guidance navigating it. There is zero shame in seeking help—it's actually a sign of wisdom and self-respect. Humans are social creatures; we heal and grow in community. Even reading memoirs or blogs by people who overcame burnout can make you feel supported and remind you that transformation is possible.
6. **Embrace Mindfulness or Spiritual Practices:** Since burnout and breakdown are as much spiritual crises as physical ones, **nurture your inner life**. This could

be through mindfulness practices like meditation, breathwork, or gentle yoga—which help calm the frazzled nervous system and create mental clarity. Even 10 minutes a day of sitting quietly and breathing can start to reconnect you with yourself. Or you might pray or engage in the spiritual practice of your tradition, seeking strength and insight from a higher power as you understand it. Many people in times of breakdown find solace in things like journaling (as we did above), reading inspirational texts, or spending time in nature as a form of meditation. These practices remind you that **you are more than your circumstances**. They tap into the part of you that is eternal, wise, and connected to the greater universe. This can bring profound peace amid chaos and spark intuitive ideas for your next steps.

7. **Take Breaks and Renew Your Environment:** Sometimes, a short-term fix can have long-term effects. If possible, allow yourself a **real break** from your routine. This could mean using some vacation days to have an open, unscheduled week. Or it could be a weekend getaway to a quiet place. A change of scenery often shifts perspective. While a single vacation won't *cure* burnout by itself (studies show the benefits of a vacation can fade in a few weeks if nothing else changes), it can be an important **reset button**. Use the time to rest deeply—sleep, sit in the

sun, do simple enjoyable things. And also use it to reflect (gently) on what your life could look like if it felt more balanced and vibrant. Sometimes stepping out of the daily grind, even briefly, gives you a bird's-eye view of your life. You might return with fresh determination to make changes, or at least with your stress dialed down enough to think clearly again. If a big vacation isn't feasible, even a staycation with a rule that you *don't* do any work or chores can help. Combine any break with the other strategies above for a more lasting effect.

8. **Experiment with Small Changes:** As you start to recover energy, begin making **small experiments** toward the life you want. Change doesn't usually happen in one leap; it's a series of small steps and course corrections. If you're burnt out by your job, maybe you volunteer a few hours doing something you love, just to feel that spark again. If you're bored and craving adventure, take an online class in a subject that intrigues you or try a new social activity. If you feel a call towards a completely different career or lifestyle, dip your toes in—talk to people in that field, start a side project, or dedicate a weekend to that pursuit. These experiments achieve two things: (1) They give you **data** and experience—you'll learn more about what energizes you and what doesn't. (2) They reinforce the truth that **you are not stuck**. There are

always new paths and possibilities, and you have the power to explore them. As you accumulate small wins or insights, your breakthrough—the bigger change—will start to take shape almost naturally.

Through all these steps, practice **self-compassion**. Treat yourself with the same kindness you'd offer a dear friend who was going through a hard time. There will be days when you slip back into old habits, or days when you feel progress is too slow. That's okay. Healing and transformation are rarely linear; they loop and spiral. Give yourself credit for every effort you make on your behalf, every time you choose to rest instead of pushing yourself, every time you speak up rather than stay silent, every time you dare to dream of a better life. These are significant acts. Bit by bit, they transmute pain into power—the power to change your life from the inside out.

From Breakdown to Breakthrough: Your Soul's Upgrade

Remember the metaphors: the seed must crack, the butterfly must struggle out of the cocoon, the light finds its way through the fractures. **Your life is doing the same**. The boredom you feel may be carving out space for creativity. The burnout you're healing from may be teaching you the value of balance and self-care, so that in your next chapter you live much more vibrantly.

The breakdown that shook you may have cleared away illusions and brought you face-to-face with your authentic self—the *you* that is stronger, wiser, and more compassionate than before. In hindsight, many people come to regard their breakdown as a profoundly *sacred time*, even though it was painful, because it set them on the path they were meant to walk.

If you're not yet seeing the breakthrough, that's okay. **Trust the process you're in**. Little by little, you will notice changes: new ideas, new energy, perhaps new opportunities arising once you start honouring yourself. Keep listening to your soul's whispers and also to the **world around you**—often when we declare internally that we're ready for change, synchronicities begin to happen. You might meet someone who offers you a project or job in an area you love. Or a book falls into your hands that gives you exactly the guidance you needed. Remain open and curious. Life has a way of supporting us when we commit to living more truthfully.

In the end, **"You came here for more than a schedule."** You came here for growth, for love, for expression, for the full adventure of being alive. If your routine has cracks now, it's because you are ready to **expand beyond it**. Embrace these cracks as evidence of life happening *for* you, not just to you. Feel the fresh air and light streaming in. **This is your breakthrough in progress.** It might still feel like a breakdown today, but hold the vision that something new is being born through this process—a more **awakened you**, and a life that truly fits who you have become. In time, you will look back and see the truth of it: that the breakdowns and boredom were in fact brave and necessary breakthroughs, and that each crack in the familiar was really a **doorway** to your next, more luminous phase of life.

Your soul is upgrading—and *you* are ready. Step through the door. Welcome the light. The journey of your transformation continues, one conscious, courageous step at a time.

10

PERMISSION TO PAUSE—RECLAIMING SILENCE, STILLNESS, AND SOUL SPACE

The universe is not outside of you. Look inside yourself; everything that you want, you already are.

—Rumi

Life today often feels like a race against an endless clock. We rush from one task to the next, our calendars packed to the brim. In a world that glorifies being busy, ***slowing down can feel almost impossible****. Yet deep inside, a gentle voice whispers that you came here for more than a schedule. You have a celestial calling—a purpose far greater than checking items off a to-do list. To hear that calling, you must sometimes do the most radical thing:* ***give yourself***

permission to pause*. This chapter is an invitation to reclaim silence, embrace stillness, and create space for your soul. In these pages, we'll explore how rest can be a sacred practice that reconnects you with your true self and your greater purpose.*

The Busy Trap and the Lost Soul Voice

Picture a young professional named **Ava**. Every morning she jolts awake to her phone's alarm, immediately skimming emails and messages before she's even out of bed. Her days are a blur of meetings, commutes, and multitasking—lunch is gulped down while answering work calls, and evenings disappear in a haze of social media scrolling and last-minute errands. Ava prides herself on productivity; she feels **useful** and *needed* when every moment is scheduled. But at night, when the lights are off, she often senses a hollowness, a subtle ache. It's as if an important part of her is knocking from within, asking for attention. She ignores it, thinking *"I don't have time for that now. Maybe later."* And so the cycle continues.

Many of us live like Ava. We wear **busyness like a badge of honour**, measuring our worth by how much we accomplish each day. We fear that if we slow down, even for a moment, everything might fall apart. Society tells us *time is money, idle hands are the devil's workshop, you snooze, you lose.* We absorb these messages until we believe that **constant doing** is the only way to be valuable. In the process, we inadvertently turn away from the *voice of our soul.* That voice often speaks softly in moments of quiet—moments we have shut out with noise and activity.

Why We Resist Rest

If you've ever felt uneasy when faced with an empty evening or a quiet weekend, you're not alone. **Why is rest so hard for us?** Paradoxically, taking a break can feel uncomfortable, even scary, when we're not used to it. We might resist stillness because:

- **Cultural Conditioning:** We are taught to believe that productivity is the measure of a life well-lived. Doing nothing feels "unproductive," and we equate rest with laziness. The truth, however, is that *rest is a productive act of self-care and renewal.* Just because our society moves at breakneck speed doesn't mean our souls can keep up without pause.
- **Fear of Missing Out or Falling Behind:** In competitive environments (school, work, social media), slowing down can trigger a fear that others will outpace us. We worry, *"If I pause, will I miss an opportunity or lose my edge?"* In reality, stepping back can bring the clarity and creativity needed to leap forward. As the saying goes, sometimes we must **slow down to speed up** in a more meaningful direction.

- **Distraction from Discomfort:** Constant busyness can be a way to avoid facing deeper feelings or issues. Silence can be intimidating if we suspect that buried emotions, worries, or truths will surface in the quiet. Many people unconsciously stay busy to outrun anxiety, sadness, or questions about their life's direction. Facing these can be daunting, but remember that *the feelings we avoid in stillness are often the very ones that need gentle attention to heal.*
- **Guilt and Self-Worth:** Some of us feel **guilty** when we rest, as though we haven't "earned" a break. We might tie our self-worth to how much we do for others or achieve in a day. If we stop, we fear we're being selfish or useless. Yet consider this: **we are human beings, not human doings**. Your worth is not defined by your productivity. You are inherently worthy—busy or at rest.

Acknowledging these reasons is the first step to overcoming them. It's natural to feel discomfort when breaking the habit of constant doing. But every time you honour a pause, you're affirming that your well-being matters and that your life is more than a checklist.

The Sacred Nature of Stillness

Across cultures and spiritual traditions, **silence and stillness are often seen as sacred**. There's a deep knowing shared by monks in monasteries, sages in the mountains, and anyone who has spent a quiet morning watching a sunrise: **in stillness, we touch something divine**. When the noise of everyday life fades, the voice of the soul becomes clearer. Some call it intuition, others call it the voice of God or the higher self. Whatever your belief, *there is wisdom in the quiet spaces within you.*

Think of the **pause between musical notes** in a melody. Without the pause, the music would be a frantic jumble of sound. It's the spaces *between* the notes that give the music its soul. In the same way, moments of pause in our lives give shape and meaning to all the action. **Stillness is not empty; it is full of guidance and insight**, if only we allow ourselves to listen.

Consider an old proverb that says: *"Silence is the language of God."* In the hush of a quiet moment, you may sense your own heart speaking to you—offering clarity on a problem, a gentle nudge toward a dream you've ignored, or simply a wave of peace that reassures you that you are held by something greater. This is the **soul space** we so desperately need: a space where the mind calms and the deeper currents of wisdom can be felt.

Metaphysically, stillness is often seen as a state where we align with the flow of the universe. Instead of swimming frantically against the current, we float, **supported by a force larger than ourselves**. Ideas and solutions can arise "out of the blue" when we're in a relaxed state—have you ever noticed how insights often pop up while taking a shower, strolling in nature, or drifting off to sleep? That's the power of a quieted mind. When we stop pushing so hard, our **receptivity** increases. We become open to messages our rushing mind might have blocked out.

Psychologically, regular periods of intentional rest help our brains process and integrate our experiences. During stillness, the mind can sift through the noise and find patterns or meaning. Our nervous system shifts from fight-or-flight mode into a calmer state. In this calm, stress hormones decrease, and *healing mechanisms activate*. In fact, **rest is known to boost creativity, memory, and emotional resilience**. Taking time to pause isn't just *nice*, it's necessary for our mental and emotional health. It's like hitting the "reset" button on an overheated engine.

A Story of Transformation in the Quiet

To truly understand the transformative power of slowing down, let's look at a story of someone who found clarity in stillness. Meet **Jordan**, a creative soul with a lifelong dream of writing a novel. For years, Jordan's life was filled with obligations: working a demanding job, caring for family, keeping up with social events. The novel lived only in the corners of Jordan's mind, gathering dust. *"One day* *when things are less crazy, I'll write,"* Jordan often thought. But that "one day" never seemed to come. There was always another deadline, another favour to do, another urgent email pinging late at night.

Then, life intervened. Jordan hit a wall of **burnout**—a complete physical and emotional exhaustion that could no longer be ignored. What came next was not something Jordan would have chosen: an enforced break. Due to the burnout and stress-related health issues, Jordan's doctor insisted on a medical leave from work. At first, the sudden space in the schedule felt jarring and uncomfortable. Waking up with **nothing on the agenda** for the first time in decades was disorienting. Jordan even felt *guilty* and *anxious*: "Am I letting everyone down? Will everything fall apart without me?"

The first couple of weeks, Jordan mostly slept—long, deep sleeps that were years overdue. Then something interesting began to happen. In the quiet afternoons, sitting on the porch with a cup of tea and nowhere to rush off to, Jordan's mind started to wander in a pleasant, unexpected way. **Fragments of a story** began to surface—little character ideas, bits of dialogue, a vivid scene set by the ocean. At first they came in whispers. Jordan kept a gentle promise: no pressure, just jot it down if it comes. And so, in that **still, unstructured time**, the novel that had been waiting in the wings for so long finally found its way onto the page.

Day by day, as Jordan gave himself permission to remain in that **cocoon of rest**, not only did his physical strength return, but a deeper transformation took place. He discovered that his creativity bloomed in the spaciousness of a slow morning. He noticed the colours of the sunset again, felt the joy of doing one thing at a time. Perhaps most importantly, Jordan realised that *the world didn't end when he stepped back*. The office survived without him, and his family adapted and even grew more independent. In fact, he returned to work a few weeks later with **renewed energy and fresh ideas**, astonishing his colleagues with a calm focus they hadn't seen in him before. The novel manuscript was not finished yet, but it was well underway, and now Jordan fiercely protects a little quiet writing time each day, even amidst life's busyness. The pause that burnout forced upon him turned out to be a **blessing in disguise**—a chance to realign life with what truly mattered.

Jordan's story is just one example. You might have heard of people who leave their hectic routine for a silent retreat or even just a weekend in the mountains without wifi, and how it utterly refreshes their perspective. **Moments of pause can bring breakthroughs**. It might not require a dramatic burnout or a trip to the Himalayas; even small pauses woven intentionally into daily life can lead to meaningful shifts. The key is understanding that *rest and stillness are not obstacles to success or happiness—they are essential ingredients*.

Wintering: Nature's Lesson on Rest

When looking for wisdom on the importance of rest, **nature is one of our best teachers**. Consider the seasons: no plant blooms all year round. The trees in a forest go through cycles of growth and dormancy. In winter, a tree appears to do nothing at all—no leaves, no visible growth. To an outsider, it might seem "inactive." But under the surface, that tree is very much alive, conserving energy and strengthening its roots. Come spring, it will bud and bloom brilliantly, precisely because it honoured the season of rest.

This cyclical process is often referred to as "**wintering**." As author Katherine May describes in her work on the subject, *wintering is the act of embracing those fallow periods of life*, the times when we must step back, slow down, or even endure a cold, dark season of difficulty. It is not a failure to **pause**; it is a **strategy for survival and growth**. Think of a field that lies fallow for a season—the farmers intentionally do not plant anything new, allowing the soil to replenish its nutrients so that the next harvest will be abundant. Our lives have similar seasons. **We all have periods that feel like winter**, where life invites us (or forces us) to be still, to rest, to heal, and to reflect. If we embrace these times instead of fighting them, we prepare the ground for a vibrant spring within our souls.

Next time you feel guilty for taking a break, remember the **wisdom of winter**. Realise that rest is not only natural; it's *required* for anything—or anyone—to thrive. Just as you wouldn't yank a sprout from the ground in January and berate it for not flowering, you shouldn't punish yourself for needing periods of quiet. **Your inner winter is sacred.** It's a time to nurture yourself in invisible but powerful ways.

PART 3

STILLNESS, SOUL SPACE

THE DEEP OCEAN OF YOUR MIND

You don't find peace by
rearranging the world,
but by diving deep
beneath its noise—into
the stillness that was
always within you.

—Eckhart Tolle

Another calming metaphor for stillness is to imagine **your mind as an ocean**. On the surface of the ocean, there may be chaos—waves crashing, storms whipping up foam. This is like the surface of our mind when we're caught in stress, hurry, and endless thought loops. But if you dive down a few meters, the water is calmer. Go deeper still, to the ocean floor, and a profound quiet and stability reign. The ocean's depths remain largely undisturbed by the weather at the surface.

Your consciousness has depths just like this. **Beneath the choppy waves of everyday worries and to-do lists lies a place of inner calm**—your own deep ocean of wisdom, peace, and presence. Practices like meditation, deep breathing, or simply moments of intentional stillness help us dive below the surface turbulence. In that deep space, even if just for a few minutes, you can rest in the **tranquility of your true self**. From there, you can observe the waves at the surface without being tossed around by them.

When you return to the surface—as we all must to live our daily lives—you bring a bit of that calm with you. Stillness doesn't mean the absence of challenges any more than the ocean depths stop the storm above; it means finding an **anchor within** so that external storms don't capsize you. Remember this whenever you feel overwhelmed: *there's a deep place inside you that is always peaceful.* Giving yourself permission to pause allows you to visit that inner sanctuary and recharge.

Creating Your Soul Space: Practical Tools for Intentional Pauses

Embracing stillness doesn't necessarily require a complete life overhaul or moving to a mountaintop. **Small, intentional pauses woven into your day can make a huge difference**. Here are some practical tools and ideas to help you create moments of pause and reconnect with yourself:

- **Sacred Morning Ritual:** Begin your day with a few minutes of intentional quiet *before* you check your phone or email. This could be as simple as sitting by a window with your coffee in silence, taking a few deep breaths, or writing in a journal. Think of it as tuning your instrument before the day's symphony begins. Even **5–10 minutes of a calm morning ritual** can set a peaceful tone for the whole day.
- **Mindful Breathing Breaks:** Our breath is a built-in pause button. A couple of times a day, deliberately step away from whatever you're doing (yes, the work can wait a moment). Close your eyes and take **slow, deep breaths**. Inhale for a count of four, hold for four, exhale for six or eight—find a rhythm that feels relaxing. Even 3–5 cycles of mindful breathing can reset your nervous system and clear your mind. This is a mini-meditation you can do anytime, even at your desk or in your car (parked, of course!).

- **Digital Detox Moments:** Our devices keep us in a state of constant stimulation. Try carving out specific times to disconnect from technology. For example, choose an "offline hour" in the evening to turn off your phone, step away from the computer, and engage in a calming activity (read a book, take a bath, stretch, or just do nothing and daydream). Likewise, consider a **digital Sabbath**—perhaps one evening a week or a Sunday morning where you avoid social media and emails entirely. Notice how time feels different when it's not sliced into notifications. Initially it might feel odd or you might feel "itchy" to check your phone, but with practice these pauses become liberating.
- **Nature Walks and Outdoor Pauses:** Nature has a way of **restoring stillness inside us**. Take a short walk outside with the intention of simply observing and breathing, not going anywhere in particular. Leave your headphones behind and tune into the natural sounds around you—the wind in the trees, bird calls, the crunch of your footsteps on the ground. Even in a city, you might find a park bench or a tree to lean against for a few minutes. Let yourself just *be* there, without needing to accomplish anything. These little nature pauses can feel like pressing a refresh button for your mind and soul.
- **"Do-Nothing" Time:** Schedule an appointment with yourself that is literally for "nothing." It could be 15

minutes of lying on the couch, staring at the ceiling, letting your thoughts drift. Or maybe sitting on the porch with a cup of tea, with no agenda whatsoever. If guilt or thoughts of "I should be doing something productive" arise, gently remind yourself that *rest is productive in its own way.* This unstructured time is where creativity often sparks and where your body and mind truly relax.

- **Journaling or Mind Dump:** If your mind is racing, sometimes stillness is hard because our thoughts are loudly vying for attention. In such moments, try a quick "mind dump" on paper. Write out whatever is cluttering your head—worries, tasks, ideas—free form, without aiming for perfection. This practice can create mental space. After writing, sit for a minute in the quiet. You might find it easier to settle into stillness once the mental chatter has been acknowledged on the page.
- **Bedtime Wind-Down Ritual:** Just as you start the day with intention, try ending it with a calming routine. It could be gentle stretching, listening to soft music, or a few minutes of meditation or prayer. Dim the lights, and let the last part of your day be free from screens. This not only prepares you for better sleep (the ultimate rest), but also gives you a pocket of peace at day's end to reflect and just *exist*, rather than consume more information or entertainment.

- **Saying No and Setting Boundaries:** A practical but profound tool for creating space in life is the word "*no.*" Give yourself permission to decline additional commitments that drain you. You don't have to attend every event or help with every project. Protecting some downtime on your calendar is a valid and necessary practice. When you say no to something not essential, you are saying **yes to the pause** and yes to yourself. Your time and energy are precious resources; spend them wisely on what truly matters, and that includes your own rejuvenation.

These tools are **suggestions, not requirements**. You might start with one that resonates and gradually try others. The goal is not to add another "to-do" to your list called "relax" (that would be counterproductive pressure!). Instead, approach these ideas playfully and gently. *Which one calls out to you?* Perhaps tomorrow morning you'll step outside for five quiet minutes of sunrise watching, or tonight you'll read a poem instead of Twitter. Each small intentional pause is like a gift you give your soul.

Reflection and Journaling Prompts

Slowing down can sometimes reveal the inner barriers we have—the beliefs or fears that keep us from resting. Self-reflection is a powerful way to explore these. Take some time to journal or think about the following prompts. There are no right or wrong answers. Let your thoughts flow honestly:

- **Pause and Notice:** *When was the last time I allowed myself to truly pause?* Describe how it felt. If it's hard to remember, reflect on what a peaceful moment *could* look like for you.
- **Identify the Resistance:** *What thoughts or fears come up when I consider slowing down and resting?* Do I hear a critical voice saying I'm lazy, or a fear that I'll miss out on something? Write down those beliefs. Seeing them on paper helps you question whether they're really true.
- **Origins of Busyness:** *Where did I learn my attitudes about rest and work?* Did your family, culture, or role models send messages that constant work equals virtue? Sometimes understanding the source of our work ethic (or workaholism) can help us gently untangle from it. You might realise, for example, that you equate being busy with being *worthy* of love or respect.
- **Envisioning Stillness:** *What might become possible in my life if I embraced more stillness?* Consider the positive outcomes: Could you feel more calm, more connected to yourself and others? Might you rediscover a passion, like Jordan did with writing, or simply enjoy life more deeply? Let yourself dream on

paper about the gifts stillness could offer you.

- **The Voice Within:** *What do I sense my soul is trying to tell me lately?* This can be a tricky question if you haven't paused in a while. But take a breath and see if any quiet longing or inner knowing arises. Perhaps your soul is whispering that it needs more play, or that a relationship needs attention, or that you're ready for a change. Write whatever comes, even if it's just a few words or images. These could be clues to your next step when you make space to listen.

As you explore these prompts, remember to be **compassionate with yourself**. If strong emotions come (like sadness over how hard you've been on yourself, or anxiety at the thought of doing less), allow those feelings to be expressed. They are valid parts of your journey. Journaling itself can be a form of rest—a way to release mental tension and make room for inner calm.

Embracing the Pause Without Guilt

Even with all this understanding, you might still feel a twinge of guilt or discomfort when you try to slow down. **That's okay.** Emotions and habits don't change overnight. The important thing is to not let guilt be the boss of you. Instead, approach it with curiosity. Next time you're resting and a voice in your head says "You should be doing something more productive," calmly respond to that voice. You might say (internally or out loud): "*It's alright. There is time for everything I need. In this moment, my job is to rest. This is productive in its own way.*"

Remember that taking care of yourself enables you to take care of your responsibilities and loved ones in the long run. You cannot pour water from an empty cup. By refilling your own well, you'll have **more to give** when the time comes. This is why airlines tell us to put on our own oxygen mask before assisting others—if you're gasping for air, you're in no position to help anyone else. In life, *rest is your oxygen mask.* It sustains you so that you can fulfil your roles and dreams without burning out.

If you feel discomfort in stillness because you're not used to it, treat it as you would any new exercise. At first, it might feel awkward or even difficult. But each time you practice, you build a "rest muscle." Start small and celebrate any progress. Did you sit quietly for five minutes today? Wonderful! That's five minutes more than nothing. Were you able to take a short walk without your phone, even though you felt weird not checking it? Great—you're breaking new ground in giving yourself permission to just *be.* With time, those five minutes might become ten, and those uneasy feelings will likely transform into craving these precious pauses.

Be patient and gentle with yourself. It's natural for feelings to surface when you slow down. You might have tears one day as you finally let yourself relax (sometimes our bodies release pent-up stress through crying—it's a healthy release). You might have bursts of joy on another day when you notice how blue the sky is or how good it feels to breathe deeply. All of it is valid. Let whatever comes up in the stillness be there without judgment. You are holding space for your soul's expression, and that is a beautiful act of self-love.

Also, know that you're not alone in this struggle. Many people are waking up to the realization that **the constant grind isn't sustainable**. There's a reason you see terms like "mindfulness," "burnout recovery," and "slow living" trending. Culturally, we are yearning for a shift. By choosing to give yourself permission to pause, you're part of a quiet, powerful revolution against the burnout culture. *You are choosing a more soulful path*, one that honours balance and inner well-being.

Your Celestial Calling Beyond the Schedule

As we close this chapter, let's circle back to the idea that *you came here for more than a schedule*. Your life is not meant to be a series of appointments and obligations with your true self squeezed into the margins. **Your celestial calling—the deeper purpose of your life—needs room to breathe.** When you allow silence and stillness into your routine, you create a sanctuary where that purpose can make itself known.

Take a deep breath. Exhale slowly. There is magic in this moment of peace you've cultivated by reading these words. Your soul thanks you for it. As you step forward, may you carry the wisdom of stillness with you—a gentle compass pointing you home whenever life starts pulling you off course. **You have permission to pause, always.**

11

THE SACRED MESS—EMBRACING THE IN-BETWEEN WHERE GROWTH HAPPENS

The soul always knows what to do to heal itself.
The challenge is to silence the mind.

—Caroline Myss

I remember a time when my life felt like it had fallen apart. One year ago, I walked out of a secure job with nothing else lined up. On my last day, I packed up my desk feeling equal parts liberated and absolutely terrified.

The steady paycheck, the daily routine, the knowing what each day would bring—all of that was gone. In the weeks that followed, I woke up without an alarm clock and without a plan. Instead of relief, I felt an unexpected wave of anxiety.

My days stretched out like a blank canvas, and I had no idea what to paint on it. Friends would ask, "So, what's next for you?" and I'd force a smile and admit, "I'm not sure yet." Inside, though, not being sure felt like walking in a dense fog with no sign of the sun.

That period was what I now call my **in-between**—the limbo after an ending and before a new beginning. Some days I felt a spark of excitement about endless possibilities; other days I was overwhelmed by doubt and regret.

One moment I'd be journaling optimistically about starting a creative project or exploring a new career path. The next moment I'd be curled up on the couch wondering if I'd made the biggest mistake of my life. It was disorienting to have my old identity—the "successful professional with a stable job"—suddenly gone. Without that title or routine, I felt like a puzzle missing a piece. I was in a mess of uncertainty, and nothing I did could rush the clarity I so desperately wanted.

What I didn't realise at the time was that this void was quietly working on me. With my old schedule and labels stripped away, I was left with a raw truth: who am I when I'm not "productive" or sure of my next step?

In that uncomfortable open space, I began to discover parts of myself I had long ignored. I started writing in my journal just to make sense of the chaos, and out poured dreams I had shelved for years.

I took long walks without a destination and sometimes found myself moved by simple things—a quote on a street poster, a memory from childhood, the way the sunrise painted hope across the morning sky.

Slowly, I realised that **not knowing** was not the enemy I thought it was. It was an invitation to know myself beyond a job title or a role. Looking back now, I see that the messy in-between was not a detour from my path; it *was* my path. It was a sacred pause, a necessary cocoon phase before the next chapter of my life unfurled.

The In-Between: A Sacred Space for Growth

Every life has these periods of **in-between**, when one chapter has ended but the next has yet to begin. It might come after quitting a job, ending a relationship, graduating from school, moving to a new city, or experiencing a major identity shift. On the surface, these transition times can feel chaotic or empty. We often label them a "mess" or a "rut." But beneath the surface, something profound is taking place. Just like a seed in the dark soil or a caterpillar in a cocoon, **you are growing in ways you can't yet see**.

In many spiritual traditions, the **void** or liminal space is considered sacred. It's seen as the fertile darkness from which new life emerges. Think about the stillness between an inhale and exhale, or the winter season when fields lie fallow. In those quiet in-between moments, there is renewal happening under the surface. Life's transitions are no different. When one aspect of our life dissolves and the new has not yet formed, we are in the womb of transformation. It's not an empty void at all, but a place of **unmanifest potential**—a soul-level incubation period preparing us for the growth to come.

It can be hard to appreciate this when you're in the thick of it. Our society celebrates certainty and constant productivity; taking time in the unknown can feel like falling behind. We're used to measuring progress by visible markers—new jobs, new relationships, clear goals. So when we find ourselves in a gap with nothing concrete to point to, we often feel like something's gone wrong. But I want to assure you: **nothing is wrong with you** if you're in this space. In fact, this "nothing is happening" phase is often when the most important growth is happening. Your soul knows the value of the pause, even if your mind is impatient. The messy middle is an essential part of the journey, not a detour. It's where old parts of you are shed and new insights take root.

Remember, you came into this life for more than just checking off boxes on a to-do list. **You came here for more than a schedule**, and that means your growth won't always follow a linear calendar or a five-year plan. The universe, or whatever guiding force you believe in, often works in cycles and seasons, not straight lines. That in-between stretch where you feel "nothing" is happening might actually be the very terrain where your **celestial calling** starts to reveal itself. When you embrace that truth, the void becomes less intimidating. It becomes a place of **possibility**—a sacred ground where the seeds of your next chapter are quietly germinating, getting ready to break through and bloom when the time is right.

Why We Resist Uncertainty

If embracing the in-between is so important, why do we struggle with it so much? The answer lies partly in our psychology. As human beings, we're wired to seek security and understanding. Our brains love knowing what's coming next—predictability helped our ancestors survive. When we don't have clear answers or a defined identity, it can trigger a primal fear. **Uncertainty feels threatening** to our mind because it's like walking through a dark room, not sure where the furniture is. In response, we often try to grab onto something—*anything*—that gives a sense of control or clarity. We might rush into a new job or rebound relationship just to escape the discomfort of not knowing. Or we obsessively overthink scenarios, trying to mentally forecast a future that hasn't arrived. All of this is our attempt to reduce the anxiety that ambiguity brings.

Another reason we resist the unknown is that our identities get wrapped up in what we do and the roles we play. If you've always been known as the dedicated teacher, the reliable manager, the spouse or parent—any label—suddenly being *between* roles can feel like an existential crisis. You wonder, "Who am I, if I'm not that?" Our ego panics when it can't latch onto a clear identity. It's as if a part of us fears we might disappear or lose our value if we aren't **being something definable**. Couple that with societal pressures—people asking for updates, the expectation to always have a plan—and it's no wonder we feel uneasy. We're culturally conditioned to prize certainty and quick answers, so sitting in uncertainty can even carry a sense of shame or failure, as though *not* knowing is a mistake. But this couldn't be further from the truth. Feeling lost or unsure is not only normal; it can be profoundly constructive if we allow it to be.

Learning to Embrace Not Knowing

So how do we find comfort in the discomfort? How can we navigate these in-between times without losing our minds or forcing ourselves into premature decisions? It starts with a shift in perspective. **Not knowing is not an absence—it's an open space.** When you think of uncertainty as a blank canvas rather than a dead-end, you reclaim some power and possibility. Instead of saying

"I have no idea what's next, this is terrible," you might say, "I'm in a place where anything could happen, and I'm open to discovery." This isn't about pretending to enjoy the uncertainty when you don't; it's about gently training yourself to see the unknown as a curious friend rather than a vicious enemy.

One powerful approach is **acceptance**. This doesn't mean you *like* feeling uncertain; it means you acknowledge it without fighting it. Instead of expending energy trying to escape the void, allow yourself to be in it. You might remind yourself, "Okay, I am in a transition. It's natural to feel unsettled. I can accept that this is where I am right now." When you stop resisting, a strange thing happens: the fear starts to loosen its grip. You realise that you *can* coexist with uncertainty and still be okay. In fact, by leaning into the not knowing, you might feel a bit of release—there's nothing to fix in this moment, only things to feel and observe. Practices like mindfulness or meditation can help with this, because they train us to sit with what *is*, without constantly reaching into the future. Even simply taking life one day (or one hour) at a time, focusing on what you *do* know (like "Right now I can make a cup of tea and breathe"), can anchor you when your mind starts spinning stories about an unknown future.

Another key is **trust**. Trusting yourself, trusting the process of life, and if it resonates with you, trusting a higher power or divine timing. This means believing that the answers will come in their own time and that *not* having those answers right now might actually be for the best. Imagine planting a seed: you don't dig it up every day to see if it has sprouted, right? You water it, give it sunlight, and trust that nature will take its course. Similarly, in a transitional period, you can do your best to take care of yourself and create a supportive environment, but you also have to trust that **clarity will bloom when it's ready**. Many spiritual teachings tell us that the universe or our soul often works on a timeline different from our ego's schedule. There is a bigger picture unfolding. What feels like a delay or a mistake might simply be the Universe arranging pieces behind the scenes. When you trust this, you begin to relax into the unknown, knowing that there is meaning taking shape even if you can't see it yet.

Nature's Metaphors of Transformation

When life gets confusing, it helps to look at the natural world for reassurance. Nature is full of examples of that **in-between** stage that looks like a mess but is actually a crucial part of transformation. Here are a few powerful metaphors to remind you that growth is often hidden in the chaos:

- **The Cocoon Phase:** Consider the transformation of a caterpillar into a butterfly. From the outside, a cocoon looks like a lifeless, wrapped-up leaf hanging from a branch. It might even seem like nothing is happening or that the caterpillar is gone for good. But inside that cocoon, a miraculous (and messy) process is underway. The caterpillar actually dissolves into an almost liquid form, breaking down completely before reorganisation into a butterfly. If you were to peek midway, you'd see goo and confusion, not the graceful wings that will emerge. In the same way, when your life feels like it's dissolving into chaos, it may be because you're in the middle of forming something new. **Without the cocoon phase, the butterfly never gets its wings.**

- **Fallow Fields:** Farmers know that soil needs to rest. After seasons of planting and harvest, a field is sometimes left fallow—nothing is planted for a time. To an onlooker, a fallow field might look wasted or unproductive: just bare earth lying there, unused. But in that supposed "empty" time, the soil is regenerating. Nutrients are being restored. The land is becoming fertile again so that future crops can grow healthy and strong. Our lives have seasons like this too. You might feel like "nothing is happening" and panic that you're wasting time. Yet it could be that this is your season of restoration. **Your inner soil is replenishing**—getting you ready for the robust growth to come.

- **The Cracked Shell:** Think of a baby bird hatching, or a seed breaking open underground. From the perspective of the shell, things are literally falling apart. The shell cracks and splits, ceasing to be the protective home it once was. If you only looked at the broken shell pieces, you might think something was destroyed. But in truth, that cracking is an act of creation. It allows new life to step forth. The chick emerges into the world; the seedling sprouts toward the sun. In our lives, the "shell" can be a comfort zone or old identity that we've outgrown. When it starts to crack, it can feel like you're breaking apart. But **a cracked shell means a new life is starting.** The discomfort and fragmentation are what allow you to emerge more fully as your next self.

Practical Tools for Navigating Transitions

While every person's journey is unique, there are some practical approaches that can support you during a transitional period without rushing you to a false finish line. Consider trying a mix of the following tools and see what resonates with you:

- **Mindfulness and Meditation:** Set aside a few minutes each day to sit in quiet or focus on your breath. Practices that keep you in the present moment can prevent your mind from racing too far into an unknowable future. This can be as simple as a 5-minute breathing exercise in the morning or a calming meditation when anxiety about the future spikes.

- **Journaling:** Writing out your thoughts and feelings can be incredibly clarifying and cathartic. Use a journal to vent your fears and hopes, or to explore questions. (If you're not sure where to start, try some of the reflection prompts later in this chapter.) Journaling helps you process emotions and often reveals insights lurking beneath the surface.
- **Routine & Ritual:** Create a gentle daily routine or small rituals to give yourself a sense of stability. This might be a morning walk, a cup of tea in the afternoon while reading something inspirational, or a nightly gratitude list. A bit of predictable structure in your day can be comforting when larger aspects of life feel up in the air.
- **Creative Expression:** Engage in a creative activity purely for joy or exploration. Paint, write poetry, play music, garden—anything that lets you express yourself without any pressure to produce something "useful." Creativity can be a form of active meditation and can channel the energy of uncertainty into art or play.
- **Seek Support:** You don't have to navigate the in-between all alone. Reach out to friends, family, or a mentor who can listen without judgment. Sometimes

just sharing what you're going through with a compassionate listener eases the burden. If you feel the need, seeking guidance from a counsellor, life coach, or spiritual advisor can also provide reassurance and tools for coping.

- **Self-Compassion:** Above all, be kind to yourself. Pay attention to your self-talk during this time. When you catch yourself being self-critical for not having everything figured out, imagine how you'd speak to a dear friend in your situation. You'd likely be encouraging and gentle, right? Offer yourself that same understanding. Remind yourself that it's okay to be a "work in progress." In truth, we all are.

Reflection Questions for the In-Between

Take some time to explore your own "sacred mess" through reflection or journaling. You can write your answers in a journal or simply ponder them quietly. These prompts are designed to help you find meaning in your current transition and perhaps see it with new eyes:

- **Where are you in transition right now?** Describe the area of life where you're experiencing an in-between phase. What chapter has closed (or is closing), and what unknown or new beginning are you facing?
- **How do you feel in this void space?** Write down the emotions that come up when you think about

not knowing what's next. Are you scared, excited, frustrated, hopeful? All of the above? Name and acknowledge those feelings.

- **What might be gestating beneath the surface?** Even if you can't see any progress, what do you sense could be forming within you during this time? Are there new interests, ideas, or aspects of yourself that have quietly emerged since you entered this transition?
- **Recall a past transition that led to growth.** Can you think of a time in your life when you went through a period of uncertainty and it eventually worked out or taught you something valuable? What happened, and what did you learn from that previous "messy middle"?
- **How are you handling uncertainty (and could you allow it more)?** Notice your tendencies: Do you find yourself rushing to make decisions or clinging to any hint of certainty? What would it look like to surrender control just a little and trust the process you're in? Is there something you can do to feel a bit more comfortable with not having all the answers right now?
- **What support or self-care can you lean on?** Identify ways to nurture yourself during this time. For example, are there small daily rituals that give you comfort, people you can talk to, or creative outlets you can explore while you wait for clarity? How can

you remind yourself that this in-between phase is temporary and meaningful?

- **If your future self or a wise guide could speak to you now, what might they say?** Imagine yourself a few years down the line, or envision a loving, wise presence comforting you. Write a short note from them to you, reassuring you that things will fall into place. What encouragement or advice do they give you about this moment in your journey?

Affirmations for Patience and Trust

Words carry energy, and what we say to ourselves matters. Try repeating or writing down the following affirmations to help you stay centred during uncertain times. These **soul statements** are meant to encourage acceptance of the mess, patience with the process, and trust in the divine timing of your life. Speak them aloud or in your heart, and feel their meaning:

- I am exactly where I need to be right now.
- I trust the divine timing of my life and know that everything unfolds when the time is right.
- I release the need to have all the answers today. It's okay not to know; clarity will come in its own time.
- I embrace this in-between space as a sacred part of my journey, knowing it is leading me to growth.

12

SOUL GPS—FOLLOWING YOUR INTUITION WHEN LOGIC FAILS

Everything in your life is there as a vehicle for transformation. Use it!

—Unknown

Have you ever faced a crossroads where every logical sign pointed one way, yet a quiet voice inside whispered something different? Maybe you had a secure job offer with a good salary and benefits—on paper, the obvious choice—yet your gut tugged you in another direction. Or perhaps all your friends said a certain relationship was perfect for you, but deep down you sensed something was off. In those moments, it can feel like you're torn between a map of reason and an inner compass that defies explanation. That

- I choose patience with myself and the process. I give myself permission to grow at my own pace.
- Even in this mess, I am learning, healing, and evolving every day.
- I am guided and supported, even when I can't see it. I trust that I am not alone on this path.

Embracing the sacred mess means understanding that this confusing in-between is not a sign of failure or a void to escape, but a vital part of your soul's evolution. Try to be gentle with yourself in this space. Give yourself permission to not have it all figured out. You are growing in ways you might not comprehend yet. When the next chapter of your life arrives—and it will, in its due time—you will step into it with the deeper wisdom and strength that you cultivated here in the uncertainty.

Remember that every hero's journey includes a passage through the unknown. This is your passage. It's where you shed what no longer serves you and prepare for what will. Trust that just as the stars align in the sky, the pieces of your life are aligning too. In the meantime, you are not idle; you are becoming. Your **celestial calling** is unfolding even now, in the sacred mess of the in-between. And when you emerge, you'll carry the sacredness of this journey with you, shining brighter than before.

inner compass is your **Soul GPS**, *and it often knows the way forward when logic comes up short.*

When Logic Falls Short: A Story of a Guiding Whisper

I want to start with a personal story that taught me the power of intuition. A few years ago, I found myself stuck in a job that, logically, was a dream come true. I had a steady paycheck, a clear career ladder, and the approval of my family and peers. By all external measures, I *should* have been happy. But inside, I felt an uneasy stirring—an inexplicable sense that something was missing.

Each morning as I sat in traffic on the way to the office, a small voice in my mind would whisper, "This isn't where you're meant to be." It made no logical sense. I had worked hard to get here and success was within reach if I just stayed the course. So, for months, I ignored that whisper and tried to reason it away. "Everyone feels this way sometimes," I told myself. "Maybe I just need to be more grateful." I kept pushing down the discontent and sticking to the *safe plan.*

As time went on, the feeling only grew stronger. It was like having an internal GPS that kept insisting I take an exit off the highway, even though my road map (and everyone around me) said to keep going straight.

I remember one afternoon, after a particularly restless

day at work, I took a walk during my lunch break. I wandered into a bookstore, seeking a distraction. A book practically fell off the shelf in front of me—it was about finding one's purpose. Coincidence or not, the word *purpose* jumped out at me. Flipping through the pages, I felt that quiet inner voice whisper again, telling me there was a different path waiting.

My logical mind interjected: "Quit the job? Are you crazy? You have bills, responsibilities. You can't just follow a feeling." Fear chimed in too: "What if you fail? What if you regret giving up this security?"

For weeks I felt caught in a tug-of-war between my *head and my heart*. On the surface, I continued my routine, but internally I was negotiating with myself every day.

The turning point came one Sunday night when the familiar anxiety about Monday morning was building up. I sat down with my journal, desperate to make sense of the turmoil. Without overthinking, I started writing about what I truly wanted in life. To my surprise, the pen moved almost on its own, spelling out dreams I hadn't allowed myself to admit: my passion for working with people more directly, my longing for creativity and freedom, my desire to make a difference beyond meeting quarterly targets.

It was as if my soul was speaking on the page, laying out a map of what could be. *None of it* fit neatly into the logical career plan I was on, yet it felt truer than anything my rational mind had come up with.

That night, I made a pact with myself: I would start trusting this inner guidance, even if it scared me. It didn't mean I would recklessly quit the next day, but I committed to exploring the alternate route my Soul GPS was suggesting.

Over the next few months, I quietly started taking steps guided by intuition. I enrolled in an evening course that had intrigued me for years, even though it wasn't directly related to my job. I reached out to a former colleague who was doing community-based work I found inspiring, just to learn more. Each small step felt exciting and a little scary—but a *good* scary, if that makes sense, like I was on the right track.

My logical brain still objected from time to time ("Are you sure about this? What's the end goal here?"), but I noticed something interesting: the more I listened to my inner voice, the more everything around me seemed to align.

I met people who encouraged me and offered opportunities out of the blue. My evening class rekindled a joy in learning I hadn't felt in ages. Even my day job became more bearable, because I knew it was no longer a trap—it was now a stepping stone, funding my transition toward a more fulfiling path.

Eventually, the day came when I handed in my resignation. It was both terrifying and exhilarating. I didn't have every detail figured out (much to my planner brain's dismay), but I had a clear sense that I was finally on the path meant for me. My intuition had guided me to start my own small coaching practice and devote more time to writing—things that *truly* lit me up. In the months that followed, there were challenges and moments of doubt, but never once did I regret listening to that initial whisper. Every time I felt lost or unsure, I turned inward and that same quiet guidance would nudge me forward: *keep going, you're getting warmer.*

Looking back, if I had only listened to logic, I might still be on that well-paved but unfulfiling road, wondering what else was out there. By daring to follow my Soul GPS, I discovered a life that feels authentic and purposeful. This experience taught me that intuition often sees truths that logic can't yet grasp. It's like having a personal navigation system attuned not to the shortest route or the most practical one, but to the *most meaningful journey.* Sometimes we have to be brave enough to diverge from the map everyone else is using and trust the compass within.

Reflection: *Can you recall a moment in your life when you had a gut feeling that defied logic? What happened when you listened—or when you didn't? Keep that example in mind as we explore how intuition works and how you can tune into it more deeply.*

The Nature of Intuition: Your Soul's Language

What exactly *is* intuition, and why does it sometimes seem to know more than our rational mind? On a practical level, intuition is often described as a gut feeling or an inner knowing that doesn't come from conscious reasoning. Psychologists might say it's your subconscious mind noticing patterns or picking up on information faster than your conscious brain. But on a metaphysical level, many see intuition as the *voice of the soul* or the whisper of the divine, guiding us toward our true path. Both perspectives can coexist: perhaps your soul communicates through those subtle feelings, using the subconscious mind as its translator.

Think of intuition as a language beyond words. It often speaks in sensations, imagery, or quiet hunches. Sometimes it's that sudden feeling of certainty about a choice, even when you can't explain *why* you feel that way. Other times, it might be a physical sensation—like a heaviness in your stomach when you're about to do something that isn't right for you, or a sense of lightness and excitement when you're considering a positive opportunity. Some people experience intuition through synchronicities (meaningful coincidences) or vivid dreams that later come true. These are all ways your inner self might be communicating. It's a bit like having an inner radar attuned to your personal truth, scanning the horizon for what aligns with you.

However, society doesn't always encourage us to trust this inner radar. From a young age, many of us are taught to "stick to the facts," "be reasonable," and rely on external guidance—whether it's what the experts say, what's written in a book, or simply *the way things are done*. We get used to planning our lives according to formulas and schedules. Logic and analysis are certainly valuable tools, but they have limits. Logic is based on the information our brain knows and the assumptions it makes. Intuition, on the other hand, can tap into a broader field of understanding—including things we haven't consciously learned or that can't be measured on a chart. Have you ever just *known* something about a person upon meeting them, before any evidence was available? Or had a flash of insight about a problem that came out of nowhere while you were taking a shower or daydreaming? That's intuition at work, often when the busy mind steps aside for a moment.

Metaphysically speaking, you can imagine that your soul has a bird's-eye view of your life's journey. It can see the terrain ahead—the opportunities, the detours, the purpose you came here to fulfil—much like a satellite guiding a GPS. The soul then sends signals to your conscious self in the form of intuitive nudges to help you navigate. This might sound mystical, but even if you take a more scientific angle, the idea holds: your brain is processing far more data than you are consciously aware of, and it can alert you to things that your conscious mind hasn't recognised yet. In either case, there's *wisdom beneath the surface* of our usual awareness.

Learning to understand this soul language starts with noticing it. Intuition often *whispers* rather than shouts. It's subtle and easily drowned out by the noise of overthinking, stress, or outside opinions. If you're not paying attention, you might miss the gentle tug in your heart or the quick thought that flits across your mind. The good news is that intuition is a skill we can nurture. It's not a gift reserved for a few; everyone has an inner guidance system. The more you acknowledge and act on it, the stronger and clearer its signals become. It's like exercising a muscle or tuning an instrument—you refine it through practice and trust.

One common question is, "How do I know if it's really my intuition speaking and not just random thoughts or wishful thinking?" The first step is to *slow down* and listen. Intuition resides in the present moment, so when you're multi-tasking or rushing, it's hard to pick up on it. Creating little pockets of stillness in your day—a few deep breaths, a quiet walk, a moment of mindfulness—gives your intuition a chance to surface. In those moments, pay attention to your body and your emotions. Intuitive insight often comes with a sense of clarity or peace, even if it suggests doing something courageous or unexpected. In contrast, thoughts that stem purely from worry or bias might feel jittery, loud, or conflicted. We'll delve more into distinguishing intuition from fear in the next section.

Fear vs. Intuition: Telling the Difference

It's important to clarify the difference between an intuitive nudge and a fear-based reaction, because they can feel strangely similar at times. Both can manifest as a strong inner voice or feeling pushing you one way or another. How can you tell if an urge to avoid something is your intuition warning you, or just anxiety playing tricks? How do you know if the excitement you feel is genuine inner guidance or perhaps an impulsive whim? Here are some clear distinctions to help you discern the two:

- **Quality of Feeling:** Intuition, even when alerting you to take caution, tends to have a calm, clear quality. It feels like a gentle knowing or a *soft* whisper that says "this is right" or "something is off here," without panic. Fear, in contrast, often feels loud, chaotic, or heavy. Fear shouts while intuition whispers. For example, you might feel a quiet but firm gut feeling not to trust a particular situation; it's not hysterical, just clear. Fear, however, might manifest as a pit in your stomach accompanied by racing thoughts of worst-case scenarios. If you feel a sensation of dread that comes with a barrage of "what if" thoughts, that's likely fear talking. Intuition's messages feel more centered in the present moment ("this is what's true right now"), whereas fear catapults you into future disasters or replays past hurts.

- **Emotional Tone:** Intuition is often neutral or positive in tone, even if it's guiding you away from something. It might feel like relief, clarity, or even a subtle excitement about a new possibility. Fear-based reactions carry a negative or frantic emotional tone—anxiety, desperation, anger, or confusion. Let's say you get an idea to apply for a job in a completely different field. An intuitive surge might come with a spark of inspiration and an "oddly certain" feeling that you should give it a shot. A fear response, on the other hand, would immediately flood you with worry: "Don't even try, you'll fail, it's too risky!" The former feels empowering or illuminating, while the latter feels limiting.
- **Persistence vs. Obsession:** Intuition often comes as a subtle insight that gently returns to your awareness if you didn't act on it the first time. It's patient. Fear is impatient and often obsessive; it will spin you in circles. For instance, your intuition might quietly suggest a few times that you reach out to a certain old friend. If you don't, you'll notice the thought popping up again here and there—always gently reminding. Fear-driven thoughts, in contrast, might grip you and not let go, repeating incessantly ("Call them right now or else something bad will happen!" or "If you don't do this, everything will fall apart!"). Intuition invites, whereas fear demands and naggingly harasses.

- **Physical Sensations:** Your body can provide clues. Intuitive guidance can manifest as a calm, relaxed alertness in the body. You might feel "in flow," or get goosebumps, or feel your heart open up. Fear typically triggers stress responses—tense shoulders, a knot in your stomach, a racing heartbeat, or shallow breath. Imagine standing at an opportunity's door: intuition might feel like butterflies of excitement mixed with a strange serenity, whereas fear feels like your stomach dropping out and pulse skyrocketing in panic.
- **Focus of Thoughts:** Intuition is often simple and matter-of-fact. It presents a notion or direction without a long story. Fear comes with a dramatic narrative. If you find yourself constructing elaborate scenarios of doom or overanalyzing every angle, that's likely fear hijacking your mind. Intuition might just say, "Go this way," or "Not this." It doesn't usually explain itself with a 10-paragraph essay in your head. Fear will try to convince you with lots of arguments (often inconsistent ones at that).

Example: Imagine you are considering moving to a new city. An intuitive nudge might manifest as a calm clarity one morning that "It's time to move," accompanied by a subtle excitement and an inner peace about the decision—even though it's big and scary. There may not be a logical reason, but it feels right. Fear, conversely, might show up as either extreme doubts ("You'll ruin everything if you go!") or even as false excitement masking panic ("Yes, do it right now because you need to escape your current problems!"). Intuition isn't about escape; it's about alignment. If the thought of moving is intuitive, it will feel aligning, like puzzle pieces clicking into place. If it's fear-driven, it might feel like running away or grasping at straws.

It's worth noting that sometimes fear can initially *camouflage* as intuition, especially if we're emotionally charged or have unresolved trauma. For example, if you've been hurt in a past relationship, your fear might scream "Run!" whenever you get close to someone new, claiming it's a "gut feeling" that this will end badly. But if it's truly intuition warning you, it usually won't come from a place of unresolved past pain; it will come from a grounded sense in the now. One way to discern is to check: *Am I reacting to something happening here and now, or to a story from my past or future worries?*

When in doubt, give it a little time. Intuition can withstand patience—if it's true, it will remain clear or even grow clearer after you sleep on it. Fear often loses some of its grip with time, or jumps to a new worry du jour. By waiting a day or two (when possible) and revisiting the feeling, you may notice intuitive guidance is steady, whereas fear is fickle or fades.

Story—A Lesson in Telling the Difference: A friend of mine once had to decide whether to accept a promotion that involved moving abroad. She felt a lot of anxiety about it and nearly declined the offer, thinking her discomfort was an intuitive sign not to go. But when she sat with it, she realised the "no" voice in her head was full of catastrophic what-ifs and memories of a past move that had been hard. That was fear talking. Beneath that, when she took a few deep breaths and got honest, there was a quieter feeling—one of excitement and curiosity about the new country. That quieter feeling was her true intuition saying "yes, this is right, if you're brave enough." She eventually took the promotion and it turned out to be a life-changing, positive experience, despite some challenges. It wasn't that her intuition was telling her "this will be easy"; it was simply guiding her to the path her soul needed for growth. Fear tried to keep her "safe" by avoiding any discomfort, but intuition led her toward fulfilment.

Strengthening Your Soul GPS: Practical Tools

Like any skill, connecting with your intuition gets stronger with practice. Think of it as tuning into a radio frequency—at first it might be staticky, but with the right adjustments you hear the music loud and clear. Here are some practical tools and habits to help you strengthen your **Soul GPS** and make listening to your inner guidance a natural part of your life:

- **Mindfulness and Meditation:** One of the best ways to hear your intuition is to *quiet the mental chatter.* When your mind is constantly analyzing, worrying, or replaying scenarios, it's like trying to hear a whisper in a loud room. Meditation doesn't have to be complicated—just sitting quietly for a few minutes a day, focusing on your breath or even doing a simple activity like walking in silence, can create space for intuitive insight to arise. As you practice mindfulness, you'll become more aware of subtle thoughts and feelings that flit through your awareness. Those subtle whispers are often your Soul GPS giving directions. If traditional meditation is hard for you, try any activity that helps you enter a calm, present state: gardening, painting, taking a shower, gentle stretching. The key is to give your mind a chance to pause and listen.
- **Journaling and Reflection:** Writing is a powerful way to engage with your inner voice. When you journal, you bypass some of the conscious filters that normally guard your thoughts. Try this: write a question at the top of a page, something you want guidance on, such as "What do I need to know about this situation?" Then, without forcing it, let your pen flow with whatever words come. Don't overthink or censor it. You might be surprised at the insights that spill out. This is often called "free writing" or "intuitive journaling." Another approach is to dialogue with

yourself on paper—write a concern or fear that's on your mind, then respond to it from the perspective of a wise, loving inner voice. It might feel like you're imagining what a supportive friend or a higher self would say. That *higher self* voice is your intuition speaking through the page. Re-reading past journal entries can also show you how often your gut feelings were right, which builds trust in your Soul GPS.

- **Body Listening:** Your body is an antenna for intuition. Practice tuning into it. Take a moment right now, close your eyes if you can, and recall a situation when you felt truly happy or "right" about something. Where in your body do you sense that feeling? Maybe your chest feels warm, your face smiles, or you get a feeling of lightness in your stomach. That's how your body says "yes." Now think of a time you felt a strong "no" or a warning about something. How does that register physically? Perhaps a tightening in your gut or shoulders, a sick or heavy sensation. This simple check-in exercise helps you learn your body's unique language for intuition. When you need to make a decision, actually pause and ask your body: how do I feel about option A? And option B? Notice the physical responses—they might be subtle at first, but with practice you'll start discerning your *yes*, *no*, and *not now* signals. Some people even use a technique called the *sway test*: stand up, calm your mind, and think of a statement like "Taking this job is in my best interest." If your body subtly sways forward, it's as if your body is leaning into a yes; if you sway backward, it could indicate a no. It's a way to involve your body's wisdom in the decision.

- **Practicing with Small Decisions:** If trusting your intuition on big life choices feels daunting, start small to build confidence. Play little games with your intuition during your day. For example, when you're going out to eat, pause and check which menu item you *feel* drawn to before even reading all the details. When driving or walking, occasionally ask your inner guidance which route to take and see if it leads you to discover something new or avoid traffic. If you suddenly feel like calling a friend or family member for no obvious reason, do it and note what happens (often you'll find they were just thinking of you, or you end up having a meaningful conversation). These might seem like trivial things, but each time you follow a small intuitive nudge and see a positive or intriguing result, you're essentially *training yourself* to recognise and trust that voice. It builds a track record that you can then rely on when bigger intuitions arise.
- **Creating a Supportive Environment:** It's hard for intuition to flourish in a chaotic, negative, or overly busy environment. While we can't always control everything in our lives, do what you can

to create spaces and moments that are conducive to inner listening. This could mean setting aside a corner of your home as a peaceful "reflection spot" with calming décor, or it could mean starting your morning with a few minutes of silence before grabbing your phone. It might involve spending more time in nature, where the natural calm can attune you to yourself. Also, consider the people you discuss your dreams and worries with: share with those who honour intuition too, or who at least respect that inner exploration. Skeptics have their place (they can keep us balanced), but if you're trying to build your intuitive confidence, you don't need constant eye-rolls or "that makes no sense" commentary from others. Protect your budding intuitive choices like you would nurture a small plant—give them some sunlight and gentle care, especially at the beginning.

- **Ask for Signs or Guidance:** If you're open to a bit of mystical play, you can literally ask your Soul or the Universe for a sign. This is a tool many spiritual seekers use to strengthen faith in their inner guidance. For example, you might say, "If I'm meant to take this path, show me a clear sign." People often choose a symbol that's meaningful to them—a certain animal, a song, a number—and then stay open to seeing if it appears in an uncanny way. While we have to be careful not to read too much into every little coincidence, clear signs can and do show up when invited. Whether you see these as messages from a higher power or just your own heightened awareness picking up patterns, it ultimately reinforces that you're being guided. I remember once I was torn about moving to a new city and I asked for a sign to guide me. I chose a random symbol—a white feather—something I wouldn't normally expect to see often. Over the next week, I kept finding white feathers in the strangest places, including one on my doorstep. It felt like a gentle nudge that my intuition about moving was on track. These experiences can strengthen your trust that there's more at play than sheer logic.

By practicing these tools, you create a kind of dialogue with your Soul GPS. At first, it might feel like you're speaking into the void or making things up, but over time you'll likely notice that intuition becomes more tangible. Remember that patience is key. You wouldn't expect to play beautiful music the first time you pick up a violin—similarly, give yourself grace as you learn the instrument of inner guidance. Some days will feel like you're deeply connected, and other days you might feel totally out of touch (that's normal for everyone, even seasoned intuition practitioners!). The aim isn't perfection; it's consistency and genuine openness.

Your Inner Compass vs. External Maps

It takes courage to prioritise your inner compass over the external maps that everyone else seems to swear by. An external map can be anything from societal expectations and cultural norms to well-intentioned advice from friends and family or the analytical pros-and-cons list you make for a decision. These "maps" are often created from collective logic about what one *should* do in a given situation. While they can be helpful references, they are general by nature—they're not tailored to your unique journey. Your Soul GPS *is*.

Imagine a sailor navigating the seas before modern instruments. They might use maps and compasses, but in uncharted waters or when storms hit, they'd turn to the stars or their own sense of direction to guide them. In the journey of life, your intuition is like that North Star. It can guide you when the usual markers (like logic and social approval) aren't sufficient or are pointing in the wrong direction for you. There will be times when following your inner compass makes you feel like you're going against the grain. You might have people in your life questioning you: "Are you sure? This isn't what you normally do," or "But everyone else is doing it *this* way." It can be uncomfortable to trust yourself in those moments. But remember, every great explorer or innovator, every person who's lived a deeply fulfiling life, at some point had to trust an inner calling that others didn't immediately see or understand.

This book is called *Your Celestial Calling—You Came Here for More Than a Schedule* precisely because it's about breaking free from living life strictly by the schedules, formulas, and checklists that society hands us. Your life's purpose isn't a task list, and your inner guidance knows that. Schedules and plans have their place (they help us organise and take action), but they are meant to serve your deeper calling, not suppress it. If you've ever meticulously planned something—be it a career path, a wedding, a personal project—only to have unexpected detours lead you to an even better outcome, you'll know what I mean. Sometimes the *unplanned* moments contain the magic. Intuition thrives in those unscripted spaces.

Let's be clear: using your Soul GPS doesn't mean throwing logic out the window entirely or refusing all guidance from the outside. It's about *balance* and *alignment*. Think of logic as one tool in your navigation kit, and intuition as another. When they work together, you're both informed and inspired. For example, if you feel intuitively drawn to start a business, logically you'd still do research and planning to support that intuition. But if some research says "this is a hard field" yet your gut continues to glow at the idea, you wouldn't abandon the idea just because the statistics look daunting—you'd acknowledge that your soul might be drawn to this challenge for a reason. Conversely, if logic presents a very convenient opportunity but your inner voice gives a clear "no," you'd take that seriously rather than dismissing it because "the numbers look good."

There's a saying: "*Intuition is a sacred gift and the rational mind is a faithful servant.*" Problems arise when we elevate the servant above the master. Your rational mind should serve your soul's goals, not sabotage them. The magic happens when you let intuition lead and then allow logic to fill in the details—rather than letting logic dictate and leaving your intuition in the backseat. As you practice listening inwardly, you'll likely find that life becomes more guided, sometimes in ways that save you from trouble or open doors you never even knew existed.

If you're ever unsure or feeling swayed by outside voices, come back to centre. Take a quiet moment and affirm: *My inner compass knows what's best for me.* Imagine literally holding a compass in your hand that points to *your true north*—that's the direction of your purpose and authentic joy. Others might have maps that worked for them, or projections of their own fears and hopes, but your true north will not steer you wrong if you have the courage to follow it.

Journaling Prompts for Inner Guidance

To truly integrate the lessons of this chapter, it helps to reflect on your own experiences. Journaling can turn abstract concepts into personal insights. Set aside some time to write about the following prompts. Be honest with yourself—there are no right or wrong answers, only your truth.

1. **Recall an Intuitive Moment:** *When was the last time you had a strong gut feeling or intuitive hunch about something?* Describe what it felt like and what outcome followed. Did you listen to it? How did things turn out? What did this experience teach you about your intuition?
2. **Logic vs. Intuition:** *Write about a situation where "logical reasoning" told you one thing but your inner voice urged another.* What did each side (logic and intuition) say? Which did you end up following, and what was the result? In hindsight, what would you do the same or differently?
3. **Fear or Intuition?:** *Think of a decision you're facing (or have recently faced) where you feel uncertain.* List any fears or anxious thoughts you have about it. Then, take a few deep breaths and ask yourself what your calm inner knowing says. Write down the messages or feelings that come when you get quiet. How do the two voices—fear and intuition—differ in this situation?
4. **Soul Communication:** *Reflect on how your soul seems to get messages across to you.* When have you felt that something greater (your higher self, the universe, God—whatever resonates) was trying to tell you something? How did the message arrive (through a dream, a coincidence, a physical sensation, a creative

idea)? Writing about past instances can help you recognise the patterns in how your Soul GPS speaks.

5. **Strengthening the Signal:** *What practices make you feel most connected to your intuition?* For instance, have you noticed that you get insights when you're in nature, or journaling, or after a good workout? Conversely, what habits seem to drown out your inner voice (e.g., constant screen time, over-scheduling, being around negative influences)? Jot down a plan for how you can incorporate more of the supportive practices and reduce the noise.

Take your time with these prompts. You might address one per day, or whichever one calls to you most. The goal is to deepen your self-awareness and to validate that *yes, you do have an inner guidance system and it has been with you all along.* By writing these things out, you create a personal dialogue with your soul.

Affirmations to Trust Your Soul GPS

Affirmations are positive statements that can help reprogram your mindset and reinforce your beliefs. To help anchor the wisdom of your intuition, try repeating some of these affirmations. You can say them out loud, write them in your journal, or simply read them silently and feel their meaning. Choose one or two that resonate strongly and make them a daily mantra:

- "I trust my intuition to guide me, even when the path is not clear."
- "My inner voice is wise and loving, and I listen to it with an open heart."
- "I am connected to my soul's guidance. My Soul GPS always leads me toward my highest good."
- "Fear may visit, but it does not control me. I choose to act from inner wisdom, not panic."
- "I release the need to have all the answers logically. I embrace the answers that come from within."
- "Every day, my connection to my intuition grows stronger. I am attuned to the subtle cues and signs guiding me."
- "Even if others don't understand my choices, I honour what feels deeply right for me."
- "I came to this life for a purpose, and my inner compass will keep me aligned with that purpose."
- "When logic fails or falters, I turn inward and find the guidance I need."
- "I have faith in my journey. With my soul as my navigator, I am never truly lost."

As you speak or write these affirmations, really envision what they mean. For instance, when you say "My Soul GPS always leads me toward my highest good," picture yourself confidently walking a path lit by an inner light, even if the world around you is dark or confusing. The more you infuse these statements with feeling, the more effective they become at shifting your mindset toward one of intuitive trust.

In Closing

Learning to follow your intuition when logic fails is like learning to navigate by the stars when the roadmaps end. It may feel unfamiliar at first, but it awakens a profound sense of freedom and trust in life. Remember that you are more than a set of checklists and external expectations. You **came here for more than a schedule**; you came with a celestial calling, a unique purpose that is revealed step by step when you tune into your Soul GPS. Embrace that inner guidance system. It is more reliable than any external map when it comes to living a life that is true to you. Each time you choose to listen and act on your intuition, you strengthen the connection between your human self and your higher self. And that connection is a lifelong compass, always there to help you find your way, especially when logic alone cannot.

Trust yourself. Your soul knows the way home.

13

YOUR WORK IS NOT YOUR WORTH—BREAKING THE IDENTITY TRAP OF TITLES AND TO-DOS

Don't be pushed around by the fears in your mind.
Be led by the dreams in your heart.

—Roy T. Bennett

"I don't even know who I am without my work." *These words echoed in Jason's mind the day after he left the company he'd devoted twenty years to. On his last morning at the office, he packed up his plaques and nameplate, feeling as though he were stripping away pieces of himself. Jason had always been the first to arrive and the last to leave, proud of his title as Director and the busy schedule that proved he was "important." But now, waking up to a* *day with no meetings and no emails, he felt an unsettling emptiness. Without the constant rush of tasks and the identity of his job, he realised he had forgotten how to just* ***be****. He stared at the mirror and saw a tired man who had poured every ounce of his being into a role that no longer existed.* ***Who was he now?*** *In that quiet and uncomfortable moment, Jason recognised that somewhere along the way, he had lost sight of his deeper self. His work had become his world—and without it, he felt lost.*

Many of us can see a bit of ourselves in Jason's story. Whether it's leaving a long-held job, facing a sudden layoff, retiring, or even just coming home at night after a busy day, the question can arise: **"Apart from my work and to-do list, who am I?"** We live in a culture that constantly praises productivity, job titles, and achievements. It's no surprise that we start to weave our self-worth tightly into what we do for a living. When someone asks, "What do you do?" we often automatically respond with our job title, as if it were a full definition of who we are. Over time, we might even forget that there's more to us than our career or daily responsibilities. This chapter is a gentle but urgent reminder: **your work is not your worth**. You are so much more than any title on a business card or any item on a to-do list. It's time to break the identity trap of titles and tasks and reconnect with the **authentic being** you truly are.

The Trap of Over-Identification with Work

It's easy to fall into the trap of over-identifying with our work. Consider a fictional example of a woman named *Aisha*. From a young age, Aisha excelled in school, and later in her career as an engineer. Every accomplishment earned her praise, and she grew to love the feeling of being needed and known for her competence. She took on extra projects, answered emails at midnight, and wore her *"busy-ness"* like a badge of honour. Her business card carried a prestigious title, and she'd often casually mention her 60-hour workweeks as if they were proof of her value. But one weekend, Aisha fell ill with a severe flu that forced her to rest. As she lay in bed with no choice but to stop doing, she felt anxiety bubbling up. She realised that without her projects and emails, she didn't know how to feel good about herself. Resting made her uneasy because she'd built her self-esteem entirely on being *productive*. In that vulnerable moment, she saw how *over-identified* she had become with her job. Aisha had conflated **who she is** with **what she does**, and it took a forced pause for her to see the cost of that mental habit.

Stories like Jason's and Aisha's illustrate *the identity trap*. This trap convinces us that our worthiness comes from our work and productivity. It's a sneaky, sticky belief that can lead us to live on autopilot, always chasing the next task or the next accolade to feel valuable. How does this happen? Often, it's a gradual process. We start by taking pride in our work (which is natural and not inherently bad), but slowly, external validation and accomplishments start to feel like the **only** measures of success in life. Society certainly reinforces this. Think about social situations: when you meet someone new, one of the first questions is likely, "What do you do?" We hear messages that equate high-paying jobs or visible achievements with being "successful" as a person. Over years, these messages sink in and form a belief that **if we're not doing something impressive, we aren't worth much**.

This mindset is further strengthened by the ego—the part of us that craves recognition, status, and a secure identity. Our ego just *loves* labels and titles. It's the ego that *puffs up* when you can say, "I'm a manager at X company," or "I'm the top performer in my department." It's also the ego that *wilts* and panics when those labels are challenged or removed. Have you ever felt a sting of insecurity when someone your age has a "better" title or when you're temporarily between jobs? That's the ego, worrying that without a shiny label, it's not sure who it is. The ego's fear-based voice might whisper, "Without your job, you're nobody. Without productivity, you're lazy or useless." These are lies, but powerful ones—and they keep us clinging tightly to work as identity.

The danger of this trap is that any change in our work situation can shatter our self-image. If your self-worth is tied to your job, then a setback at work isn't just a professional issue; it feels like a personal failure. Imagine someone who hears criticism from a boss—if they're over-identified with their work, that critique can feel like **I am a failure** (instead of *I did not meet a work expectation this time*). Or consider those who retire or lose a job; instead of seeing it as a life transition, they might experience it as an identity crisis. It's as if the ground beneath them has disappeared because the role that propped up their self-esteem is gone. This can lead to anxiety, depression, or a desperate scramble to find a new source of external validation. When work becomes *the* defining feature of who we are, we also often neglect other parts of life—relationships, health, inner growth—because all our energy is funnelled into sustaining that work identity. It's a classic **all your eggs in one basket** scenario, and that basket can be dropped at any moment.

Recognising that you've fallen into this trap is the first step to freedom. It's not about blaming yourself—after all, the world we live in actively encourages equating **doing** with **worth**. But when you become aware that you are more than your job, you start to see a glimmer of your deeper self calling out, wanting to be acknowledged and valued for *being*, not just doing. The rest of this chapter will help you answer that call.

Who Are You Without the Resume?

Take a moment to reflect: **Who are you outside of your job and accomplishments?** If you strip away the titles, the degrees, the awards—what remains? This can be an uncomfortable question if you're not used to thinking of yourself beyond your roles. It might even draw a blank at first. But this question is at the heart of breaking free from the identity trap. Another way to frame it is: "*Can you remember who you were before the world told you who you should be?*" Who were you before you started building a resume, before you began measuring your days by tasks and achievements?

Perhaps as a child, you were an explorer, an artist, a daydreamer, a kind friend. Back then, you didn't have a job title, yet you had a distinct essence. You had **interests, feelings, and a presence** that was uniquely you. Children don't worry about proving their worth; they simply *are*. If you spend time with a young child, you'll notice they find joy in *being*—playing, imagining, experiencing—without needing to justify it with productivity. Similarly, think of someone you deeply love (a friend, a partner, a family member). Do you love them because of their job title or salary? Probably not. You love them for who they are—their personality, their spirit, the way they make you feel. The same applies to you: **you are worthy of love and respect for *who you are*, not for what you do.**

Try to picture yourself standing in a room with nothing but your true self. In this visualization, you gently remove the "uniforms" of your roles. You take off the "employee" hat, the "student" badge, the "manager" name tag, the "parent" or "provider" cape—all the identities that involve doing and giving. Just set them aside for a moment. What does it feel like to stand there without those identifiers? You might feel naked or vulnerable at first, as if you've removed heavy armour that you've worn for years. There's a feeling of exposure—this is natural. But there's also a potential feeling of relief. The armour of titles and to-dos can be **heavy**. Removing it, even mentally, can feel like a weight lifting off your shoulders. You may notice a softer self underneath, one that maybe hasn't had as much attention in a long time.

This exercise of imagining yourself without your roles is a way to get reacquainted with your **authentic beingness**. Your authentic beingness is the part of you that exists beyond roles, beyond ego, and beyond external validation. Some might call it your soul, spirit, or simply your inner self. It's the *you* that observes your life, that experiences the world directly, that feels joy, pain, love, and wonder—irrespective of any job performance. That core self is inherently worthy. It doesn't earn worth through a checklist or a promotion; it **is** worth, by its very existence. This concept can be a bit abstract, so let's ground it with a metaphor:

Think of the sun in the sky. The sun shines not because someone pays it or because it won an award for "Best Star." The sun simply shines because that's its nature. It has light and warmth to share by virtue of what it is. If one day the sun decided not to rise, we wouldn't say the sun is worthless—we'd say something is off, because we know the sun's *true nature* is to shine. Similarly, your true nature is to **be** and to shine in your own way. You carry a "light"—your personality, love, creativity, kindness—that exists regardless of any task you complete.

Unfortunately, in the hustle of adult life, we often forget our inner light. We get caught in **performing** instead of **being**. We put on layers of identity like cloaks: the professional cloak, the achiever cloak, perhaps the caretaker cloak—each one may serve a purpose, but none of them is the real *you*. This chapter encourages you to start uncloaking. Remove those cloaks, bit by bit, and reacquaint yourself with the person underneath. Remember, you came into this world as a whole, complete being long before you had a resume or a to-do list. That wholeness is still within you.

So ask yourself gently: *Who am I without my job? What qualities do I have that have nothing to do with my career or productivity?* You might find answers like: "I am compassionate," "I am curious," "I am funny," "I am a good listener," or "I am a lover of nature." These are the threads of your identity that often get overshadowed when work steals the spotlight. By bringing them back into focus, you start to redefine your worth in a broader, more truthful way.

When Titles Become Armour

At times, we use our titles and busy schedules as a form of armour. Just like a knight might wear a suit of armour to protect against external threats, we use our professional identity to shield us from deeper fears. The armour of "*I am an attorney*," "*I run my own business*," or "*I am the go-to person at my company*" can feel protective. It wards off insecurity by projecting strength and importance. It can also shield us from the judgment of others—if we present an impressive front, maybe people will respect us and we'll feel safe.

However, armour is heavy and isolating. When you're always clad in the armour of your work identity, people might see the impressive exterior, but **not the real you inside**. Moreover, you might start to believe that without this armour, you're defenseless or insignificant. This belief is exactly what keeps so many people stuck in the identity trap. They fear that if they step out of their professional persona, even for a moment, they won't know how to face the world. But ask yourself: *What am I defending or protecting by over-identifying with my work?* Often, the answer lies in fear—fear of not being enough, fear of failure, fear of uncertainty about who we'd be without a structured role.

Consider a fictional character, *Nina*, who is known by everyone as a top-notch surgeon. Her title carries prestige, and she's proud of the lives she saves—rightly so. But over the years, that title also became her armour. Whenever she felt insecure or lonely, she'd remind herself of her status: "I'm Dr. Nina Matthews." It gave her a momentary boost, a sense of worth. She poured more and more of her time into work because it was where she felt competent and valued. Yet, inside that armour, Nina sometimes felt hollow. At night, she realised she barely had energy to call her old friends or pursue hobbies she once loved like music. She had gradually let the armour constrict her life. When she imagined retiring one day, it terrified her—taking off that armour felt like losing herself.

Nina's story shows how what starts as a positive passion or dedication can turn into ego armour if we rely on it too much for our self-esteem. The invitation here is not to *quit* the things you love or stop doing good work; it's to **stop deriving your sense of worth solely from them**. You can be passionate and excellent in your career and still know that *you* are more than the job. In fact, recognising this can make you even better at what you do, because you won't be operating from fear of failure or a need to prove yourself—you'll be operating from genuine inspiration and purpose.

Visualize removing your armour. This doesn't mean you abandon your skills or quit your job on the spot; it means mentally acknowledging that the armour is not fused to your skin. You can take it off. Picture unlatching a heavy breastplate labeled with your title, setting down a shield that's emblazoned with your list of responsibilities. Imagine breathing easier without it. When you remove the armour, you become more approachable, more human. You might feel more connected to others because you're allowing your true self—with all its warmth, quirks, and even vulnerabilities—to be seen. It can be scary, yes, but it is also profoundly liberating. People around you might respond positively as well; seeing someone who is confident enough in themselves *without* the armour of position can be inspiring. It shows that real confidence comes from within, not from titles.

Metaphysical Reflections: You Are a Soul, Not a Role

Beyond the psychology of it, there's a metaphysical or spiritual perspective to consider. If you resonate with the idea that life has a greater purpose or that we are more than just our physical bodies and societal roles, this section is for you. Even if you're not sure about the spiritual side, try to approach it with an open mind—sometimes a shift in perspective can come from considering something a bit beyond the ordinary.

The central spiritual reflection here is that **you are a soul on a human journey**, not a human defined by a job. The very title of this book, *Your Celestial Calling—You Came Here for More Than a Schedule*, speaks to this idea. "Celestial" implies something heavenly or star-like, and "calling" suggests a purpose or mission. Think about that: if you came here (to this life on Earth) for more than a schedule, then your true worth and purpose must transcend any daily agenda or career path. Schedules and jobs are part of the human experience, but they are not the *essence* of it.

From a metaphysical viewpoint, each person has an **intrinsic value** that comes from simply being a living expression of life, or if you prefer, a child of the divine (the universe, God, Source—however you name it). In this view, your worth was 100% on the day you were born and it will remain 100% on the day you die, regardless of how productive you were in between. No soul comes into this world with a mandate like "You must accomplish X amount of work to be worthy." Instead, the soul's goals might be things like experiencing love, learning compassion, expressing creativity, and growing through challenges. Many spiritual teachings suggest that when we look back on our lives (maybe in our final moments or beyond), what will matter most is how we **lived** and

loved, not the length of our resume.

This reflection can be empowering: if you truly believe (or are willing to believe) that you have a celestial origin and an inherent purpose, then you can start to see your job as just one avenue through which you express yourself, not the definition of your value. Your job or daily tasks become tools or playgrounds for the soul, rather than scorecards of your worth. For example, if your calling is to bring healing into the world, you might do that through your profession as a nurse or doctor—but you would also still carry that calling in how you treat your friends, how you volunteer, how you listen to a child who's hurt. The calling is bigger than the job title.

Similarly, if your celestial calling is to learn and spread joy, you might currently be doing that as a teacher or maybe as an office manager who brightens everyone's day. But if one day you change careers or roles, your true calling goes with you. You **cannot lose it**, because it's part of you. This means that if circumstances take you out of a job (or you choose to leave), you haven't lost *yourself*—you've just lost one channel of expression. There will be other channels, other ways for your soul to shine and fulfil its purpose.

Understanding this can help calm the ego's panic about changes in work or status. The ego sees a job loss or retirement as a kind of death of identity. The soul sees it as simply a change of form, an opportunity to grow in a new direction. Your ego might say, "I am a failure if I'm not working in this high-powered role." But your soul might whisper, "I am still me—creative, compassionate, whole—and I will continue to grow and touch lives no matter what outer form my work takes."

In metaphysical terms, you might affirm: *I am a divine being having a human experience.* This human experience includes work, yes, but it also includes relationships, personal growth, play, and stillness. **Spiritually, being is valued over doing.** Many meditation practices, for example, encourage one to sit in stillness and recognise that the self observing the thoughts is separate from those busy thoughts. If you've ever meditated or even just sat quietly in nature, you may have touched a feeling of "just being"—a sense that you are part of something larger, and that you are complete in that very moment without needing to achieve anything. That state is what we mean by *authentic beingness.* It is deeply peaceful and affirming.

Even if you don't identify as spiritual, you can appreciate that life's richness isn't solely determined by productivity. Think of profound moments in life: watching a sunset, laughing with a loved one, overcoming a personal challenge, or even grieving a loss—these experiences shape us and often bring out our humanity in full depth. None of them requires a promotion or a pat on the back from a boss. They're part of the journey of being human and being a soul.

So remember: **You are a soul, not a role.** Your roles (worker, parent, student, etc.) are like costumes you wear on the stage of life. You can take them off or change them, but the actor—the soul—remains. This perspective can help loosen the tight grip of identifying with any one role. It also brings a sense of safety: no matter what happens in the realm of titles and to-dos, your core self remains intact and valuable.

Practical Tools for Redefining Your Worth

Breaking the habit of tying your worth to work requires not just insight but also practice. Here are some practical tools and mindset shifts to help you start redefining your worth on your own terms:

- **Practice Self-Introduction Beyond Work:** Challenge yourself to introduce or describe yourself without mentioning your job title. For instance, if someone asks what you do, you might say, "I'm a curious person who loves painting and spending time with my family," or "I enjoy hiking and I'm passionate about animal rescue," *before* you mention the job. This might feel awkward at first, but it trains you to see yourself (and help others see you) as more than a job. It's also a great conversation starter that isn't centered on work. By putting who you *are* before what you *do*, you remind yourself that your identity is multifaceted and rich, regardless of your career.

- **Ask Others "Who Are You Outside of Work?"** Similarly, when talking to friends or meeting new people, try asking questions that aren't about their job. For example, "What do you love to do?" or "How do you spend your time when you're not working?" This shifts the focus away from defining people by their jobs. It creates space for more meaningful connections and reinforces for you, the asker, that life is about much more than work. You might be surprised how people light up when given a chance to share about their hobbies, families, or dreams.
- **Set Boundaries with "To-Dos":** Your to-do list is not a measure of your worthiness. To remind yourself of this, set clear boundaries for your work and tasks. This could mean having a cutoff time in the evening after which you don't check work email, or designating one day a week where you do very little and allow yourself to just relax or follow your curiosity. When you stick to these boundaries, notice the discomfort that might arise ("I feel like I should be doing more"). Instead of obeying that discomfort by rushing back to work, sit with it. Recognise that the uneasy feeling is just the old belief ("I must be productive to be valuable") trying to reassert itself. By not giving in every time,

you gradually train yourself to **be okay with being**, not just doing.

- **Cultivate Hobbies or Activities for Joy, Not Achievement:** Start an activity where the primary goal is enjoyment or self-expression, not performance. It could be something like journaling, gardening, playing a musical instrument, crafting, dance, or learning a language for fun. Do it as a beginner, with no pressure to be great at it. When you engage in something purely for the joy of it, you reinforce the idea that not everything in life needs to be a competition or a task. You're allowed to have aspects of life that aren't about achieving. These hobby moments reconnect you with your *curious inner child* and remind you that you have worth and identity outside of being "efficient" or "the best."
- **Spend Time with People Who Value You, Not Your Achievements:** Surround yourself with at least a few people who see and appreciate *the real you.* This could be family, old friends, or anyone who doesn't really care what your job title is—they care about your wellbeing and company. When you spend time with such people, pay attention to how you feel. You might notice that you feel more "yourself," more relaxed, or more seen for your personality and not your productivity. This is healing. It validates the truth that you are lovable and worthy just by being

you. If you realise your current social circle is *only* composed of colleagues or people who mostly talk about work, consider expanding it—maybe join a club, a community class, or a volunteer group where you can meet others in a non-work context.

- **Reframe Your Inner Dialogue:** Be mindful of how you talk to yourself about accomplishments and setbacks. If you find that you berate yourself when you're not productive (e.g., "Ugh, I did nothing useful today, I'm so lazy"), practice a reframe. You might instead tell yourself, "I needed rest today, and that's okay," or "My worth isn't defined by this checklist. I am still worthy even on a slow day." Likewise, if you achieve something great, of course congratulate yourself—but add a note like, "This is wonderful, but even if it hadn't happened, I would still be me, and I'd still be worthy of respect." The idea is to slowly untie the knot in your mind between achievement and worth.
- **Embrace Being Present:** A powerful way to experience your intrinsic worth is to practice presence. When you are fully present—whether that's enjoying a meal, taking a mindful walk, or having a deep conversation—you step out of the mental chatter about past/future and success/failure. In the present moment, you often realise that *everything is okay* and that you are enough. Consider trying mindfulness

meditation or simply a daily moment of pause. Even five minutes a day of sitting quietly and observing your breathing can begin to separate your sense of self from the whirlwind of tasks. In that quiet, you may feel a subtle but profound reassurance that **you exist, you are alive, and that is enough**.

- **Celebrate Non-Work Achievements (and Define Success for Yourself):** Broaden your definition of success. Make it a habit to acknowledge things you do that have nothing to do with work. Did you manage to finally start reading that novel? That's a win. Did you call a friend you haven't spoken to in a while? Celebrate that connection. Did you learn something new about yourself or practice patience in a tough moment? That's growth—applaud it. By valuing these aspects, you send yourself the message that being a well-rounded, caring, growing human is more important than just grinding out work projects. Consider writing a "success list" each week of moments you were proud of or grateful for that had nothing to do with your job.

Each of these tools and shifts is about retraining your mind and life to see **worth** in a more holistic way. Initially, it might feel like you're going against the grain—and in a sense, you are, because mainstream culture won't necessarily support all of this. But the more you practice, the more natural it will become. You'll start to notice a greater sense of peace and security in yourself. Work will take its rightful place in your life—important, but not all-consuming. And ironically, when you're not depending on work to supply all your self-esteem, you may find you perform with more ease and authenticity, because the pressure is off.

Journaling Prompts: Uncovering Your Beliefs About Work and Worth

One of the best ways to dig into the subconscious beliefs and gently shift them is through journaling. Set aside some quiet time with a notebook or digital document, and consider the following prompts. Write freely and honestly—there are no right or wrong answers. The goal is to uncover the hidden stories you've been telling yourself about who you are and what makes you worthy.

- **Early Messages About Work:** What messages did you receive growing up about work and success? Did your family, culture, or school imply that your worth is based on achievement? Write about specific memories or phrases you remember (e.g., being praised only when you brought home good grades, or hearing adults equate long work hours with being a good person). How have those messages shaped your identity?
- **Defining Yourself Without Titles:** If you were not allowed to mention your job or any roles (parent,

student, etc.), how would you describe yourself to someone new? Make a list of qualities, values, and passions that define you. For example, "I am creative, empathetic, funny, adventurous, a nature-lover, a truth-seeker," etc. What does this list reveal to you about who you are beyond work?

- **The Fear of Slowing Down:** How do you feel when you take a day off or have nothing on your agenda? Do you feel anxious, guilty, or restless? Write about a recent time you rested or did something purely fun. What thoughts came up during or after? (e.g., "I'm being lazy," or "I don't deserve this downtime until I finish X.") Where do you think those thoughts come from?
- **Your Reactions to Work Setbacks:** Recall a time when you had a failure or setback related to work or productivity—maybe a poor performance review, a job loss, or simply a day where you couldn't get much done. How did you talk to yourself about it? Did you feel "less than" as a person? Write about that experience and whether you might view it differently knowing what you now know—that your worth isn't tied to that outcome.
- **Who Were You Before Your Career?** Think back to when you were younger—perhaps late childhood or teenage years, before you started your current career path. What were your dreams, hobbies, or traits that

had nothing to do with a job? Do you still have any of those in your life? For instance, if you loved writing stories or being in nature, are those still part of you? If not, write about how you might reconnect with that earlier version of you. How could you honour who you were before the resume?

- **Imagining Life with No Work Labels:** Imagine you woke up tomorrow and for some reason, nobody was allowed to talk about or ask about jobs or accomplishments—how would you prove your worth or identity? Write a short scene or dialogue in this imaginary scenario. What would you want people to know about you? How would you want to spend your time? This can reveal what aspects of life you cherish beyond work.

Use these prompts as starting points. You might discover some deeply ingrained beliefs, such as "If I'm not productive, I'm not valuable" or "My identity is mostly my career." Simply becoming aware of these beliefs is progress. As you journal, you may begin to *rewrite* those beliefs into healthier ones, like "I have value even when I rest" or "My identity is multifaceted and not defined by any single role." Keep these insights visible—perhaps highlight them or write them on sticky notes—so you can remind yourself of the new perspective you are cultivating.

Affirmations and Soul Statements for Intrinsic Worth

To further reinforce this new understanding of your inherent worth, it's helpful to adopt affirmations or what we might call *soul statements*. These are positive, present-tense declarations that align with the truth of your being rather than the old conditioning. You can say them out loud, write them daily, or simply read them and let them sink in. Choose ones that resonate with you, or tweak the wording to feel more authentic. The key is that they should uplift you and reflect the idea that you are enough as you are. Here are some affirmations to consider:

- **I am worthy and valuable simply because I exist.**
  (Your worth is not something you earn; it is your birthright.)
- **My work is just one part of my life, not the definition of my life.**
  (You are a whole person with many facets, and no single role defines you.)
- **I am a human being, not a "human doing," and it's okay to just be.**
  (You give yourself permission to experience life beyond constant productivity.)
- **Even when I am still or at rest, my value does not decrease.**

(Rest is a natural and necessary part of life, and you remain deserving of good things even when you're not actively working.)

- **I release the need to prove my worth through achievements.**

  (You let go of any compulsion to constantly earn love or respect; you embrace that you are enough now.)

- **Who I am in my heart is more important than any title on my resume.**

  (Character, kindness, and authenticity are what truly matter to you.)

- **I remember who I was before any titles—that pure, creative, curious soul—and I honour that self.**

  (You stay connected to your innermost self, the real you that's always been there.)

- **Like a star, I shine by being myself, and my light is not measured by productivity.**

  (Invoking a celestial image, you affirm that your inner light is constant and not dependent on output.)

- **I am guided by my soul's purpose, which is bigger than any job or task.**

  (You trust that you have a meaningful purpose that can manifest through various ways, not just through work.)

- **I am enough, exactly as I am, here and now.** *(Perhaps the simplest and most powerful affirmation: recognising your sufficiency in this very moment.)*

As you read these affirmations, notice how you feel. At first, your ego might resist some of them if they contradict long-held beliefs. That's normal. For example, saying "I am worthy simply because I exist" might trigger a skeptical inner voice saying, "Really? Isn't that too easy? You have to *do* something to be worthy." If that happens, realise it's just the old conditioning speaking. Continue to gently repeat the affirmations that resonate most. Over time, repetition can help rewire your thought patterns. You might stick a favourite affirmation on your bathroom mirror or as a reminder in your phone so you see it often.

These soul statements are like medicine for the part of you that has felt "not enough." They reaffirm the truth that your soul has known all along but your mind may have forgotten: **that your worth is infinite and unchanging, regardless of external factors**. When you deeply believe this, an amazing thing happens—you start to approach work and goals from a place of wholeness and passion, rather than fear and need. You might still strive for excellence, but it will be because you enjoy it or feel called to it, not because you think it will make you more "worthy."

Embracing Your Inherent Worth

In breaking the identity trap of titles and to-dos, you are embarking on a journey of coming home to yourself. It's about remembering and reclaiming the truth that got buried under years of social conditioning and busyness: the truth that **you are enough as you are**. Your life is meant to be so much more than a productivity report. Yes, work can be fulfiling and purpose-filled, and there's nothing wrong with enjoying your career—but it's a distortion to believe that your career is the sum total of your value.

As you integrate the insights from this chapter, be patient and compassionate with yourself. Deeply rooted beliefs don't always dissolve overnight. You might catch yourself slipping back into old patterns—like overworking to feel good about yourself or feeling down on a lazy Sunday. When you notice that, rather than criticizing yourself, gently correct course. Remind yourself of the stories of Jason, Aisha, or Nina, and what they learned about themselves. Remind yourself of the journaling discoveries you made, or the feeling you had when visualizing taking off your armour. These reminders will help steady you.

Imagine waking up each morning with a sense of worthiness that isn't tied to your to-do list for the day. You take on the day's tasks not as a slave to them, but as a conscious creator choosing where to put your energy. If work issues arise, you handle them as best you can, but you know in your heart that **a work problem cannot dent your self-worth**. You have an inner sanctuary of self-esteem that is untouchable by external events. This is not only a relief; it's empowering. It frees you to take risks, to rest when needed, to live more authentically.

When you no longer *need* your job or any role to define you, you can finally hear the quieter voice of your true desires and calling. Perhaps you'll find yourself remembering passions you set aside. Perhaps you'll strengthen relationships, or take better care of your well-being, or explore new paths that align with your soul. The irony is, letting go of over-identification might actually lead you to work or create in ways that are even more meaningful—because they'll be driven by love and authenticity, not by a fragile ego trying to prove itself.

Your celestial calling—the reason you came to this life—was never about just clocking in and out or building a perfect resume. You came here for growth, connection, experience, and the full expression of who you really are. By breaking the chains that tie your identity to your work, you liberate that authentic self to answer the true call. You start living in alignment with the knowledge that **your worth has always been within**.

So wear your roles lightly, like comfortable garments rather than heavy armour. Give your best to your endeavors, but know when to lay them down. Nourish the parts of you that have nothing to do with productivity. Listen to your soul's whispers. And every day, remind yourself: *My work is not my worth. I am worthy, simply because I am.*

14

ALIGN, DON'T GRIND—FLOWING WITH ENERGY INSTEAD OF FORCING OUTCOMES

Your work is to discover your world and then
with all your heart give yourself to it.

—Buddha

"Alignment over hustle"*—it sounded like a nice theory, but for a long time I didn't believe it. I used to pride myself on being the hardest worker in the room. If there was an outcome I desperately wanted, my solution was always the same:* ***work harder, push more, sacrifice sleep****, and force it to happen. Years ago, in the early days of my career, I was grinding away at a new project I was passionate about. I poured in 60-hour weeks, made endless to-do lists, and* *tried to control every tiny detail to guarantee success. I was determined to* ***"make it happen"*** *through sheer effort. But instead of feeling accomplished, I felt like I was rowing upstream in a river against a powerful current. The harder I paddled, the more exhausted I became—and the shore of success didn't seem any closer.*

One evening, well past midnight, I found myself hunched over my laptop, heart racing and mind frazzled. I was surviving on coffee and anxiety, chasing a result that seemed to keep slipping further away the more I forced it. In that moment of exhaustion, something clicked: *this isn't working*. I realised that my relentless pushing was actually creating resistance. I was so tense and tunnel-visioned that I'd stopped listening to my own intuition about the project. I was grinding from a place of fear—fear that if I eased up even for a second, everything would collapse. In truth, things were already collapsing: my creativity had dried up, my joy was gone, and I was utterly drained.

Out of sheer burnout, I **surrendered**. The next day, I did something radical (at least, radical for me at the time)—I **took a break**. I stepped away from the project and gave myself permission to relax. Instead of obsessing over the outcome, I focused on recharging and doing things that made me feel good: I went for a long walk in nature, I journaled about what truly inspired me, and I allowed myself a full night's sleep. Over the following days, I gradually shifted from forcing progress to listening for guidance. An interesting thing happened once I **let go of the oars** and stopped fighting the current: new ideas and opportunities started flowing in. In a casual conversation, I met someone who had exactly the expertise I needed and was excited to collaborate. A fresh insight came to me about a simpler, more authentic direction for the project—something I hadn't seen before when I was stuck in the weeds. By **aligning with my energy**—tuning in to my inner voice and the supportive clues life was giving me—I began moving downstream. Tasks that felt impossible before suddenly happened with ease. What had been **an uphill struggle turned into a graceful glide**.

That experience taught me a life-changing lesson: there's a profound difference between **forcing an outcome** and **flowing toward an outcome**. When I "aligned" instead of "grinded," I achieved even better results with a fraction of the effort—and felt a whole lot happier doing it. In this chapter, we'll explore exactly how and why that works.

We'll look at what it means to *flow with energy* rather than fight against it. You'll discover how **vibrational alignment, divine timing, and energetic flow** can accomplish more for you than brute force ever could. We'll delve into how to recognise when you're out of alignment and practical ways to return to your natural flow. I'll share visual metaphors (like rowing downstream instead of upstream, tuning your inner instrument, and dancing with life) to help these concepts click. We'll also introduce journaling prompts for personal reflection—so you can uncover where in your life you might be "grinding" when you could be flowing. And to wrap up, we'll affirm some empowering soul statements to help you recalibrate toward **easeful, intuitive action**.

Ready to trade the grind for a more graceful groove? Let's dive in.

The Difference Between Forcing and Flowing

It's important to clarify what *"don't grind, align"* really means. Does it mean we should just sit back and wait for life to hand us things? Not quite. **Flowing with energy** isn't about laziness or giving up on effort—it's about the *quality* and *source* of your effort. Let's contrast the two approaches:

- **Forcing (Grinding) Mode:** When you're forcing outcomes, you're *pushing* at all costs. This mode often comes from **fear, impatience, or ego**. You might be working long hours out of panic that you'll fall behind, saying yes to every task out of obligation, or obsessing over controlling every detail. Forcing feels like **rowing upstream**—it's an uphill battle against the current of circumstances. You might notice you feel **tense, drained, and frustrated**. Often, no matter how hard or fast you row, progress seems minimal because you're fighting the natural flow. Signs you're in grinding mode include: exhaustion and burnout, constant obstacles or setbacks, a knot in your stomach or tightness in your shoulders, and a pervasive feeling of "*Why is this so hard?!*" Even if you do achieve the result, you're too depleted to enjoy it.

- **Flowing (Aligning) Mode:** When you're flowing with aligned energy, you're **allowing and guiding** rather than brute-forcing. This mode comes from **trust, intuition, and inner wisdom**. You still take action, but it's *inspired action* that feels in sync with a greater current. Flowing feels like **rowing downstream**—you still paddle, but the current is helping carry you along. In this state, you might feel **energized, creative, light, and in-the-zone**. Synchronicities tend to pop up: the right people, ideas, or opportunities appear "out of nowhere" just when you need them. You have a sense of timing where you act when it feels right, and pause when it doesn't. Signs you're in alignment include: a calm, focused mind, a body that feels more relaxed (maybe even excited), tasks falling into place more smoothly, and often a feeling of "*This is almost too easy—can it really be this fun?*" You still put in effort, but it **feels natural and rewarding** rather than forced and draining.

Think of the difference like **dancing with a partner**. Forcing mode is like trying to dominate the dance—yanking your partner (life) around the floor to hit every move you want, even if the music is suggesting something else. It's awkward and stiff; you might step on some toes (and certainly wear yourself out). Flowing mode is like being attuned to the rhythm and moving in harmony with your partner. You're not limp or passive—you're actively dancing—but you're also listening and responding. The result is a beautiful dance that feels effortless and joyful, because you're co-creating with the music instead of wrestling with it.

Another useful metaphor is the **tuning fork**: When you strike a tuning fork and then bring another fork of the same frequency nearby, the second fork will start resonating on its own. However, if the forks are out of tune with each other, you'll just hear dissonance. In life, when you are *"in tune"* with your goal or purpose—meaning your energy, thoughts, and actions are aligned with what you truly desire—things resonate and manifest with much less effort. But when you're out of tune (say, chasing a goal that deep down isn't right for you, or acting out of anxiety), it's like trying to force two mismatched notes; it just creates noise and friction.

So, **"align, don't grind"** doesn't mean "do nothing." It means **first align your energy and intention**, and then act—not the other way around. When you line up your inner state with where you want to go, you tap into a kind of guidance system that makes your actions far more effective. It's the difference between **inspired work** and just busy work.

Why We Try to Force Outcomes (And What It Costs Us)

If flowing is so much better, why do we so often default to forcing and grinding? There are a few deep-seated reasons:

1. **Fear and Urgency:** Many times, forcing comes from fear—fear that if we don't push, we'll fail or miss out. Our ego panics that things won't happen unless we personally struggle and strain for them. Maybe you fear that without constant effort, you won't be worthy of success or love. Fear creates a sense of **urgency and panic**; it whispers that time is running out, that you're behind, that you must control every variable *right now*. This leads to that clenched, frantic push, fueled by anxiety rather than inspiration. The irony is that fear-based urgency often causes us to make poor decisions or burn out, **actually delaying the outcome** or sabotaging it. When you act out of fear, it's like broadcasting static into the universe—the message of what you truly want can't get through clearly.
2. **Ego and Control:** Our ego—the part of us that wants to look good, to win, to be "in charge"—loves the narrative of the grind. Society often glorifies the grind, too, equating endless hustle with virtue and worthiness. We're taught that if you want something, you have to "make it happen" through sheer will.

There's a certain pride the ego takes in saying "I worked harder than everyone else for this." But the flip side is, the ego has a hard time surrendering control or accepting help. It doesn't trust that things could work out without its micromanagement. The ego also tends to fixate narrowly on a specific outcome it wants, in a specific way and timeline, and rejects anything that deviates. This rigidity means **we ignore the flow of life**—we might miss easier pathways or better opportunities because we're so laser-focused on forcing our single vision. The cost of letting the ego run the show is high stress, diminished creativity, and sometimes blowing right past the blessings that were quietly trying to get our attention.

3. **Conditioning and "Hustle Culture":** Culturally, many of us have been conditioned to equate effort with value. The mantra is *"no pain, no gain,"* and busy-ness is worn as a badge of honour. We may feel guilty if we're not constantly working or worrying about working. This conditioning runs deep: perhaps you saw your parents grind tirelessly and you learned that that's the only way to survive. Or in school and jobs, you were rewarded for overtime and "going above and beyond," even at the expense of your well-being. As a result, slowing down or allowing ease can actually feel uncomfortable—almost like we're doing something wrong. We might fear being seen as lazy or "unambitious" if we're not

visibly struggling. So, we override our natural rhythms and **push past our limits**, again and again. Over time, this leads to burnout, chronic stress, health issues, and a disconnection from our own inner guidance (because we're constantly looking outward for approval or for the next task to do).

4. **Lack of Trust (in Self and the Universe):** At its core, forcing is the opposite of trust. When we don't trust our own inner wisdom—or a higher wisdom of life—we feel we have only our brute force to rely on. If you've ever caught yourself thinking, "If I don't do this, nothing will happen," or "Everything will fall apart if I'm not on top of it 24/7," it's a sign of that lack of trust. It's understandable: surrendering control can feel vulnerable. Trusting divine timing or unseen support can feel like a risk if you're used to controlling everything. But living with zero trust means carrying the weight of the world on your shoulders alone. It's utterly exhausting. And it cuts you off from the creative cooperation of the universe. Imagine trying to sail a boat but refusing to trust the wind; you'd end up rowing the whole way by yourself. That's what lack of trust in the bigger picture feels like—endless manual labor, no assistance from the natural forces that could help carry you.

The costs of forcing outcomes are **high**: we sacrifice our health, peace of mind, and often the very joy that inspired our goals in the first place. We also limit our results. When you're grinding from fear or ego, you're in a contracted state—your vision is narrow, and your energy is low. You might achieve something through grinding, but it often feels hollow or unsustainable, or it comes with unintended negative consequences (like, you got the promotion but your health and relationships suffered). It's like forcing a puzzle piece to fit where it doesn't belong: you might jam it in, but the picture won't look right and other pieces will be squeezed out of place. **Alignment, by contrast, is about finding the right fit** where all pieces click together naturally.

The Power of Vibrational Alignment

Now let's talk about what's actually happening on an energetic level when we shift from grind to align. You've probably heard the phrase **"raise your vibration"** or **"vibrational alignment"** in spiritual and metaphysical circles. It might sound abstract, but it's essentially about the mood, mindset, and **energy frequency** you're operating on.

When I talk about energy or vibration here, think of it as the feeling tone you're carrying. Are you radiating anxiety and scarcity? Or confidence and abundance? Are you **"in tune"** with what you want to experience, or are you buzzing at a totally different frequency?

Here's a simple example: If you're forcing something out of desperation, your vibrational state is likely one of **lack, fear, and frustration**. Even if you don't say it aloud, internally you might be screaming "It's not happening yet! I'm worried it won't work out!" That energetic broadcast tends to repel the very outcome you seek, or at least blind you to seeing creative solutions. It's like trying to tune a radio to 101.5 FM but you've got the dial set at 98.7—you're not going to pick up the music on the right station.

On the other hand, when you focus on **aligning your inner state** first—perhaps by finding appreciation for what is working, cultivating a sense of optimism, or simply calming your mind and body—you start broadcasting a clearer signal. If your desired outcome has a "frequency" (for example, the feeling of success, or love, or whatever it is you're aiming for), then **feeling those emotions now** puts you on that frequency. When you're on the same wavelength as what you want, you become like a magnet for it. You'll notice resources and people gravitating to help you, because your energy is inviting rather than demanding. You might also notice you're more **creatively inspired**, as if you've tuned into a stream of ideas and intuition that wasn't accessible when you were in a lower mood.

Think of **vibrational alignment** as tuning your instrument. When an orchestra tunes up, each musician adjusts their instrument to match a reference tone. They pause to get in tune before launching into the symphony, ensuring that what they play will sound harmonious. In life, aligning with your inner truth—your values, joy, and authentic desires—is like tuning yourself to the reference of your soul. When you're in that alignment, the actions you take naturally create beautiful music in the world. When you're out of alignment, no matter how fast or furiously you play (work), the music will sound off.

A practical way to consider vibrational alignment is to **check in with your feelings** as an internal compass. Our emotions are signals indicating whether we're in alignment or not. Feeling **expansive emotions**—such as enthusiasm, inner peace, curiosity, love, inspiration—usually means we are aligned with our Higher Self or true path in that moment. Feeling **contracted emotions**—such as dread, excessive stress, anger, despair—often means something in our approach or perspective is out of alignment with our true needs or the highest outcome. (Now, this doesn't mean if you feel bad you should judge yourself; not at all. Those feelings are just information, guiding you to adjust course.)

When you catch yourself in those contracted states, instead of doubling down on forcing action, it's a cue to **pause and realign**. That might mean taking a break to do something that shifts your state (listening to music, stepping outside for fresh air, calling a friend who lifts you up). It might mean doing a quick meditation or simply sitting quietly and breathing, to get back to a calmer centre. It could also mean revisiting your "why"—reminding yourself of the bigger vision or purpose, to spark inspiration again.

One fascinating thing about vibrational alignment is how it taps into what some call **"flow state."** In psychology, a flow state is when you're so engrossed in an activity that you lose track of time and things unfold almost effortlessly—like an athlete "in the zone" or an artist painting with inspiration guiding their brush. When you align your energy, you create the conditions for flow states to occur more often. You might notice that when you work on something in a good mood, you get far more done in two hours than you would in eight hours of struggling when you're in a bad mood. That's vibrational efficiency. Aligned action is high-quality action.

In summary, **vibrational alignment** means your inner self, your emotions, and your intentions are tuned to a positive, clear frequency. From that place, forcing is unnecessary—you become a cooperative component with life. You're working *with* the universe, not against it. As a result, what you build or achieve tends to come together with less strain, and often in wonderful ways you couldn't have schemed or forced if you tried.

Divine Timing: Trusting the Right Moment

Perhaps one of the most challenging aspects of shifting from grind to flow is learning to trust **divine timing**. When we're in forcing mode, we usually have a very specific timeline in mind: "I need this outcome, and I need it **now** (or by X date)!" Our schedules and society's pressure can make us feel that everything is urgent. But part of aligning with the flow of life is accepting that **things happen at the right time, not necessarily our time.**

This is where a spiritual, larger-picture perspective becomes invaluable. The concept of divine timing suggests that there is a **greater intelligence or order** at play—whether you call it the Universe, God, your higher self, or simply the natural order of life. It's the understanding that sometimes when something isn't happening for you, it's because the conditions aren't fully ripe yet. Just as a fruit will only ripen in its season, our goals and desires often have their own seasons.

Think of a **seed you plant in a garden**. You water it, give it sunlight, and then you must wait and trust that it will sprout in its own time. You can't force a seed to grow faster by yelling at it or tugging on its sprout—in fact, that would likely kill the delicate plant. In the same way, forcing outcomes can sometimes "bruise" or disrupt the natural growth process of our dreams. **Divine timing** is like the seasons and weather that nurture the seed. There may be unseen factors developing: perhaps you need to meet a certain person, or learn a certain skill, or even let go of something, before your goal can fully blossom. It's often only in hindsight that we realise the wisdom of a delay or a detour. Maybe that job you desperately wanted would have trapped you in an unhappy career—and the "missed" opportunity cleared the way for a much better fit that came a year later. Maybe a relationship that didn't work out was actually making space for one that is far more aligned with who you've become.

Learning to **trust the process** and divine timing means reminding yourself that **"not now" doesn't mean "never."** It means embracing the idea that life is working **for** you, not against you, even when you can't see it yet. This trust isn't passive; it's an active choice to believe in a benevolent unfolding of events. It's replacing the thought "It's too late" or "It must happen now" with "I am exactly where I need to be, and things are unfolding at the perfect time."

Now, our ego absolutely hates this idea at first! The part of us that wants control will argue, "If I don't push, I'll fall behind. If I don't get it now, I'll never get it." But the more you practice trust, the more you'll notice something magical: **life often delivers something better than what you were in such a rush to grab.** By not forcing, you leave room for miracles and surprises. You also reduce your stress, which ironically puts you in a better state to recognise and seize opportunities when they do arise.

Shifting from Grind to Flow: Practical Tools and Mindset Shifts

Alright, so say you've recognised that you're currently more in "grind" mode in some area of your life. How do you realign and get back into that magical flow? Shifting your state and mindset takes practice, but here are several **practical tools and mindset shifts** to help you **return to flow and trust the process**:

1. **Pause and Breathe:** This is the simplest and most immediate tool. When you catch yourself tense and forcing—*stop*. It might seem counterintuitive to halt when you're trying to race to a result, but taking even a five-minute pause can prevent hours of wasted effort on a wrong trajectory. **Close your eyes, take a few slow, deep breaths**, and literally reset your nervous system. As you breathe, tell yourself it's okay to relax. This break interrupts the cycle of frantic energy and creates space for a new approach to emerge. Remember, **"the pause is power"**—you're not losing time; you're regaining clarity.
2. **Get Into Your Body:** Often, grinding mode means we've been "in our head" too much—analyzing, worrying, and strategizing to the point of analysis paralysis. To reconnect to flow, drop out of your head and into your body. You might stand up and stretch, do a quick exercise like a few yoga poses or jumping jacks, or go

for a brisk walk. Maybe even put on a favourite song and dance freely for three minutes. Physical movement shakes up stagnant energy and releases tension. As you move, imagine you're literally shaking off the stuck, forceful energy and inviting in a more fluid state. Sometimes while walking or showering (any rhythmic, physical activity), you'll find that **insights and creative ideas bubble up naturally**—that's a sign you're back in a flow-friendly state.

3. **Reconnect with Why:** Grinding often makes us obsess over the **"how"**—how will this happen, how can I make it happen faster, etc. To shift to alignment, reconnect with **"why do I desire this in the first place?"** Take a moment to recall your deeper intention or the feeling you're after. For example, you're grinding at work because you want financial security—but why? Maybe because it will give you freedom and peace of mind. How can you cultivate a bit of that freedom or peace right now? Or you're forcing a project because you want to express yourself and help others—that's the core joy. Are you tapping into that joy when working on it, or just stressing about perfection? By refocusing on the essence of your goal (the why), you shift from a fear-based chase to an inspired pull. The work then becomes about expressing that why, which naturally aligns your energy with what you want.

4. **Embrace "Good Enough" and Surrender Perfection:** A lot of grinding is driven by perfectionism and the need to control outcomes precisely. To find flow, practice letting go of the reins a bit. This might mean deliberately doing something less than perfectly and being okay with it—as an exercise in trust. For instance, if you're agonizing over an email or a report, give yourself a time limit and send it off even if it's not 110%. Tell yourself, "I allow it to be good enough, and I trust the chips to fall where they may." This doesn't mean being careless; it means acknowledging that you've done your part and now it's okay to **let the universe (or other people) play their part**. Surrendering control in small ways builds your muscle of trust for bigger things. It's incredibly liberating to occasionally say, "I've done what I can; I'll let this situation unfold now."
5. **Seek Joy and Inspiration:** Nothing shifts energy faster than genuine **joy or inspiration**. When you realise you've been grinding without joy, it's time to infuse some lightness. Do something that makes you happy or inspires you, even if it's unrelated to the problem at hand. It could be reading a chapter of an uplifting book, watching a funny video, playing with your pet, or calling a friend who always makes you laugh. Joy raises your vibration, which, as we discussed, aligns you with better outcomes. Inspiration might

come from exposing yourself to new ideas: attend a workshop, listen to a motivating podcast, or go to a beautiful space like a museum or nature trail. These aren't escapist distractions; they are refuelling stops. Often, after giving yourself permission to have a little fun or beauty, you return to your tasks with a fresh perspective and renewed creativity. In a state of upliftment, you might find that the solution to what you were forcing earlier now flows effortlessly.

6. **Meditate or Spend Time in Stillness:** Meditation is a direct route to alignment because it helps quiet the mental chatter and anxiety that fuel forcing. Even 10 minutes of sitting quietly, focusing on your breath or a mantra, can do wonders. If formal meditation isn't your thing, simply sit on a park bench or in a comfy chair at home, and gaze out the window. Let your mind drift without clutching onto any particular thought. The goal is to enter a state of **receptivity**. In the stillness, you might feel a sense of connection—to yourself, to something larger, or just a feeling of peace. That is you re-aligning. Some people find prayer has a similar aligning effect—not prayer in the begging, pleading sense, but in the sense of handing over your worries to a higher power and asking for guidance. It's essentially saying, "I'm open to help. I'm listening." This attitude invites grace and often, after such a session, you'll experience an intuitive nudge

or a new opportunity coming your way that helps you forward.

7. **Journal for Clarity:** Writing can be a powerful alignment tool because it externalises the jumble in your head. Try a free-write about what's bothering you or where you feel stuck—just pour it out uncensored. This in itself is a release, moving that frantic energy out of you and onto paper. Once you've vented, you can then ask yourself in writing, "What would it look like to approach this with more ease? What might I do differently if I trusted everything was working out?" Don't overthink it; let your pen flow with whatever ideas or even images come. You might be surprised at the wisdom your higher self delivers when given the chance. Sometimes I literally write to my inner guidance or to the universe with a question, and then write whatever response comes—it often ends up being exactly the advice I need to follow. (There are some journaling prompts in the next section to get you started on examining your grind vs. flow patterns.)
8. **Align with Natural Cycles:** We, as living beings, are subject to natural rhythms—daily energy cycles, lunar cycles, seasonal cycles, and for women, menstrual cycles. If you push hard at a time when your body or mind is naturally in a low-energy or reflective phase, you'll feel like you're grinding gears. Whenever

possible, plan your most demanding tasks for when you typically have more energy (for many, mid-morning or whatever your personal "peak" time is). And allow gentler work or rest during downtimes. If you notice you get a bit introspective or slow in winter, honour that by not overloading yourself in those months; use it for planning and restoration, then perhaps launch big initiatives in spring when energy rises. **Alignment includes working *with* your own body and nature, rather than against them.** When you sync with these larger patterns, you reduce the feeling of forcing and instead feel supported by a tide of energy when it comes.

9. **Practice Gratitude and "Already Enough":** A mindset shift that immediately soothes the urge to force is **gratitude**. When you're in grind mode, the focus is usually on what's lacking or not done yet. By switching to appreciation, you align with a sense of fullness. Take a few minutes to list (mentally or on paper) things that are going right or that you're thankful for—no matter how small. It could be as basic as "I'm grateful for the cup of tea I had this morning that gave me a moment of calm" or "I appreciate my friend who texted to encourage me." As you do this, notice the tension easing. Gratitude puts you in a receptive, positive state, which is essentially alignment with abundance. Similarly, affirm to yourself that **who**

you are and what you have right now is enough. This doesn't mean you'll never grow or achieve more; it simply means you choose to feel whole and sufficient in this moment. From that place, any action you take is icing on the cake, a joyful expression, rather than a desperate attempt to complete yourself or your life. This mindset of "I am already enough; my life is already enough" paradoxically opens the door for more blessings to flow in—because you're no longer acting from a place of lack.

Each of these tools and shifts helps you step out of the grind and back into alignment. Different ones will resonate at different times. You might even create a mini "Flow Toolbox" for yourself—a list of go-to activities or reminders for when you catch yourself forcing. For example: "When I feel myself getting into grind mode, I will *step outside for 10 minutes*, or *play my favourite calming song*, or *do a quick meditation*." It's like having an exit ramp off the highway of hustle, leading you back to a smoother scenic route.

Remember: The goal is not to become perfect at never forcing (we're human; we will slip up). The goal is to notice sooner when you're out of flow, and gently guide yourself back, over and over. This is a lifelong practice, and it gets easier and more natural with time. Eventually, you'll find that you spend much more time in ease and alignment, and the old grind habits simply don't have the same grip on you.

Reflection and Journaling Prompts: From Grind to Flow

Self-reflection is a powerful way to internalise these concepts. Let's turn inward now. Grab your journal or open a blank document, and explore the following prompts. There's no right or wrong answers—this is about **self-discovery**. Write freely and see what comes up. You might uncover beliefs and patterns that have been operating under the surface. Awareness is the first step to change!

1. **Where in my life am I "rowing upstream"?**—Identify one or two areas where you feel like you're forcing or grinding the most. Describe what that feels like and what outcome you're trying to push. How is this struggle affecting you physically, emotionally, and mentally?
2. **What am I afraid will happen if I stop pushing so hard?**—This prompt gets to the fear or belief keeping you in grind mode. Write out your fears uncensored. (For example: "If I ease up, maybe I'll fail, or people will think I'm lazy, or I'll miss my chance.") Seeing these fears on paper can help you question them compassionately. Are they really true? Is there perhaps

an equally likely positive outcome if you ease up (e.g., "If I ease up, I might actually come back with fresh ideas and do better")?

3. **Recall a time when I was in a state of flow.**—Describe a specific memory when you felt things clicked into place naturally—it could be a small event or a big win. What were you doing, and more importantly, how did you feel during that time? What elements do you think helped you be in flow (your mindset, environment, people around you, etc.)? This helps remind you that you *are* capable of flowing and good things have happened when you weren't forcing.
4. **What would "trusting the process" look like in my current situation?**—Bring to mind a situation where you've been forcing an outcome. Now imagine what it would look and feel like to trust divine timing and let go a little. How might you behave differently? What might you do with your time if you weren't worrying or overworking on this issue? Sometimes writing this as a hypothetical can illuminate practical changes you can make (e.g., "If I trusted it will work out, I would relax in the evenings instead of checking my email 20 times.").
5. **Where in my life do I feel fully aligned and in flow?**—It's helpful to recognise the areas (however small) where you naturally don't grind. Maybe you

feel in flow when you're cooking, or playing music, or when you're with certain people. Write about why you think flow comes easily there. What does that teach you about the conditions you thrive in? How can you bring some of those elements into the areas where you struggle? (For example, if you flow when you're creative and relaxed, can you bring more creativity or relaxation techniques into your work life?)

6. **What is one small experiment I can try this week to "align, not grind"?**—Brainstorm a practical action. It could be **doing one thing differently**: perhaps starting your day with setting an intention for alignment before diving into tasks, or taking a short mindful break every hour to breathe, or responding differently when something goes wrong (maybe saying "It's okay, there's a reason for this delay" instead of getting upset). Commit to trying that experiment for a few days and later journal about what you observed. Did things unravel when you let go a bit, or did some things actually get easier?

Take your time with these prompts. You might do them all in one sitting or spread them out over a few days. The insights you gain will be personal gold—they'll illuminate exactly where you need more flow and how you can invite it in.

Affirmations and Soul Statements for Realignment

To help reprogram your mind from a grind mentality to one of trust and flow, it's powerful to use **affirmations or soul statements**. These are positive declarations you can repeat to yourself (out loud, in your mind, or write them down) to reinforce a new belief. Choose any that resonate from the list below, or modify them to fit your voice. You can also post these somewhere you'll see them daily (your bathroom mirror, your planner, a note in your phone) to remind you to align with ease:

- I release the need to force outcomes; I allow the best outcomes to unfold naturally.
- I am in tune with the flow of life. What is meant for me comes to me with ease.
- I trust the timing of my life. Every delay is a blessing in disguise guiding me to something better.
- My worth is not measured by how hard I struggle. I am worthy even when I rest and recharge.
- I act from inspiration and inner guidance, not from fear or pressure.
- As I align with my inner truth, I create impact with grace and ease.
- I am co-creating with the universe; I don't have to do it all alone. Help and guidance are available to me.

- It is safe for me to let go and trust. Life supports me in every moment.
- I flow like water around obstacles. I adapt, I learn, and I keep moving forward smoothly.
- My energy is magnetic—when I feel good and aligned, I attract good into my life effortlessly.

When you say these affirmations, really **feel** the truth of them in your body. Even if your mind doubts at first, allow yourself to emotionally connect with the possibility that these statements are true. Over time, with repetition, they will sink in and become your new default thinking. For instance, the next time you catch yourself panicking that something isn't happening fast enough, you'll more readily remember: "Wait, I trust the timing of my life. I can breathe here; it's okay." Affirmations are like seeds you plant in your subconscious. Nurture them with repetition and sincerity, and they will grow into new, supportive beliefs.

Next time you find yourself caught in a storm of stress, remember that you have a choice. You can drop the rope in this tug-of-war and choose a different dance with life. Imagine yourself **rowing downstream**, feeling the current support you. Visualize your life as a dance floor where you and the universe are partners moving in sync. See yourself as a musician tuning to the perfect pitch, so the song of your life sounds delightful. These images aren't just pretty—they represent a very real shift in how you approach each day.

By aligning with your inner truth and soul timing, you'll find that you create far more impact than you ever did from frenzy and fear. And you'll do it with a sense of peace and fulfilment that no amount of grinding can ever buy. Your energy is your most precious resource—when you invest it wisely and align it with a higher flow, it multiplies and carries you to heights you might not have even imagined.

So as you step forward, carry this mantra in your heart: **Align, don't grind.** If you forget and start pushing the boulder up the hill again, that's okay—simply notice, smile at yourself, and step aside. Let gravity and grace take over where struggle used to be. The more you practice flowing with energy instead of forcing outcomes, the more you'll witness a beautiful truth: *when you align with life, life aligns for you.*

Remember, you are supported in more ways than you know, and you are always being gently guided toward the highest good. Trust it. Flow with it. Your celestial calling is unfolding, and you can let it carry you—with far less effort and far more magic than the old grind ever could.